CONTENTS

2

Zucchini Bread 33

Perfect Peanut Bread 34

Delicious Banana and Pecan Bread 34

'Cheesy' Biscuits 34

Great Corn Muffins 35

Apple and Cinnamon French Toast 35

Charming Challah 35

Stove-Top Cornbread 36

Chocolate Bran Muffins 36

Carrot, Raisin, and Ginger Muffins 36

Apple Crumble Muffins 37

Maple-Glazed Pumpkin Scones 37

Apple and Raisin Spiced Muffins 38

Cinnamon Buns 38

Banana Biscuits 38

Fantastic Flat Bread 39

Low Fat Chocolate Muffins 39

Ginger and Carrot Muffins 39

The Simplest Blueberry Muffins Ever 40

Nutty Cranberry Muffins 40

Whole Wheat Cornbread 40

Blueberry and Banana Muffins 41

Blueberry and Lemon Scones 41

Apple and Banana Muffins 41

Sweet Potato Muffins 42

Chocolate and Peanut Butter Muffin 42

Walnut Wheat Bread 42

Toddler's Muffins 43

Nut and Banana Muffins 43

Muffin Carrot Cakes 43

Very Berry Muffins 44

Strawberry, Almond, and Cream Scones 44

Orange and Pomegranate Muffins 44

Gluten-Free Hemp Bread 45

Pumpkin Spice Scones 45

Walnut Bread with Banana and Chocolate
Chips 45

Spiced Banana and Chocolate Bread 46

Banana, Walnut, and Chocolate Chip Muffins
46

Raisin Buns 46

Date and Banana Muffins 47

Cheese Scones 47

Pumpkin Spice Bread 47

Hot Cross Buns 48

Chocolate and Zucchini Bread 48

Vegan Biscuits 48

Dutch Bread 49

Roast Almond and Date Muffins 49

Cranberry, Walnut, and Pumpkin Muffins 49

Whole-Grain Pumpkin Muffins 50

Vegan Bread Machine Bread 50

Graham-Cracker Muffins 50

Chocolate and Walnut Muffins 51

Busy Muffins 51

Choca-Mocha Muffins 51

Chocolate Chip Scones 52

Cookies 52

Fig and Apple Bran Muffins 52

Rice Flour and Applesauce Muffins 53

Mixed Fruit Muffins 53

Fig, Apricot, and Cornmeal Bread 53

Fruit and Nut Pumpkin Bread 54

Oat Bran Muffins 54

Vegan Cakes 55

Brilliant Banana Cake 55

Very Vegan Vanilla Cake 55

Chocolate Mug Cake 55

Delicious Chocolate Cake 56

Carrot Cake 56

Crock Pot Chocolate Pudding Cake 57

Pumpkin Cake 57

Easy Applesauce Cake 57

Spiced Ginger Cake 58

Zucchini and Cinnamon Cake 58

Frosted Raspberry Blackout Cake 58

Simple Vanilla Cake 59

Lemon Genoise Cake 59

Iced Chocolate Cake 59

Apple and Walnut Cake 60

Carrot Cake 60

Perfect Pineapple Upside-Down Cake 60

Simple Apple Sponge Cake 61

Upside-Down Banana Cake 61

Choco-Banana Cake 61

Gooey Chocolate Cake 62

Carrot and Applesauce Cake 62

Banana and Chocolate Cake 62

Vegan Cookies 83

Vegan Bread

Cornbread

Time: 50mins   **Serves:** 9

INGREDIENTS

- 2tbsp. ground flax seeds
- 1 cup all-purpose flour
- 6tbsp. water
- 1 cup cornmeal
- 4tsp. baking powder
- ¼ cup sugar
- ¾tsp. table salt
- ¼ cup canola oil
- 1 cup soymilk

METHOD

1. Preheat your oven to 425°F, and grease an 8-inch square baking dish.
2. Bring the water to a boil, then add the ground flax seed and simmer for three minutes, until thickened. Reserve.
3. In a bowl, combine your cornmeal, flour, sugar, baking powder, and salt, then stir in the ground flax seed mixture, soy milk, and canola oil. Beat until smooth.
4. Bake for 20 to 25 minutes, then leave to cool in the tin for ten minutes.
5. Turn onto a wire rack, and cool for another ten minutes, then serve warm.

Easy Vegan Bread

Time: 2hrs 50mins   **Serves:** 20

INGREDIENTS

- 1½tsp. salt
- 4 cups unbleached flour
- 1 (2¼tsp.) packet active dry yeast
- 1¾ cups hot water (about 105 degrees)
- 2tbsp. extra virgin olive oil

METHOD

1. Combine the salt, flour, and yeast, then form a well in the bottom.
2. Pour your water into the well, followed by the oil.
3. Pull the flour into the liquid slowly, using a wooden spoon, until fully absorbed.
4. Work into a ball, then tip onto a floured surface. Knead for five to ten minutes, until elastic.
5. Put the dough into a large, greased bowl, and cover with a damp cloth.
6. Leave to prove in a warm place for an hour to an hour and a half. Preheat your oven to 375°F.
7. Knead again to work out any air bubbles, then divide into two round loaves on greased pans, and leave to prove for another twenty minutes. Bake in your oven for 30-40 min until the crust turns golden.

Blueberry Muffins

Time: 50mins   **Serves:** 12

INGREDIENTS

- ¼ cup margarine (soy or regular)
- ½tsp. salt
- ½ cup unsweetened
- applesauce
- 1 cup sugar
- 1tbsp. baking powder
- 2 cups flour
- 1tsp. vanilla
- 2 cups frozen blueberries
- ½ cup soymilk

METHOD

1. Preheat your oven to 350°F, and line your muffin cups.
2. Combine all the ingredients, then divide between your muffin cups, filling each ¾ of the way.
3. Bake for 35 minutes, or until the tops are firm.

Banana Bread

Time: 1hr 15mins   **Serves:** 12

INGREDIENTS

- ¾ cup brown sugar
- ½ cup margarine, softened
- ¾ cup white sugar
- 3 very ripe bananas, mashed
- ½tsp. baking soda
- 2 cups flour
- ¼ cup vanilla-flavored soymilk, mixed with
- 1tsp. vanilla
- 1tsp. apple cider vinegar
- 1tsp. cinnamon
- ½tsp. salt
- ¼tsp. allspice

METHOD

1. Preheat your oven to 350°F, and grease a 8x4 bread pan.
2. Combine your baking soda, flour, salt and spices.
3. In another bowl, cream the margarine with the sugars.
4. Stir in the soy milk, bananas, and vanilla.
5. Combine the two mixtures, then pour into your pan.
6. Bake for 60-70 minutes.

Simple French Toast

Time: 7mins   **Serves:** 4-6

INGREDIENTS

- 1 cup vanilla-flavored soymilk
- 1tbsp. sugar
- 2tbsp. flour
- 1tbsp. nutritional yeast
- 4-6 slices bread (slightly stale is best)
- 1tsp. cinnamon

METHOD

1. Combine all the ingredients but the bread.
2. Submerge the bread in the mix, then remove and cook on a skillet until golden.

Spelt Banana Bread

Time: 1hr   **Serves:** 9

INGREDIENTS

- ½ cup maple syrup
- 3 ripe bananas
- 3tbsp. canola oil
- 1½tsp. baking soda
- 1½ cups spelt flour
- ¼tsp. salt
- 1tsp. vanilla
- ¾ cup pecans

METHOD

1. Preheat your oven to 350°F, and grease a loaf pan.
2. Combine your mashed bananas with your canola oil, maple syrup, and vanilla.
3. Sift in the dry ingredients except the nuts, and combine well.
4. Fold in the nuts, then pour into your pan and bake for 42 minutes.

Banana Muffins

Time: 30mins   **Serves:** 12

INGREDIENTS

- 1tsp. cinnamon
- ½ cup vegetable oil
- 4 ripe bananas, mashed
- ½ cup brown sugar or pure maple syrup
- 1tsp. cardamom powder
- 1 cup whole wheat flour
- ¾tsp. salt
- 1½ cups white flour
- 1tsp. baking soda
- 1tsp. baking powder

METHOD

1. Preheat your oven to 350°F, and grease your muffin tins.
2. Combine your mashed bananas with the sugar or maple syrup, oil, salt, cinnamon, and cardamom.
3. Stir in the baking powder, flours, and baking soda.
4. Divide between your tins, and bake for 20-25 minutes.

Banana and Walnut Muffins

Time: 30mins   **Serves:** 12

INGREDIENTS

- 1⅓ cups wheat flour (or other flour)
- 1tsp. baking soda
- ½ cup unrefined sugar
- 1tsp. baking powder
- ¾ cup oat bran
- 1tsp. salt
- 2 over-ripe bananas, mashed
- ⅓ cup olive oil
- ½ cup chopped walnuts
- ⅔ cup rice milk
- 1tsp. vanilla extract

METHOD

1. Preheat your oven to 375°F, and grease you muffin tin.
2. Combine all the wet ingredients, then sift in the dry ingredients and mix well.
3. Divide between your muffin tins, and bake for 20 minutes.

Wheat Bran Muffins

Time: 40mins   **Serves:** 12

INGREDIENTS

- 1 cup wheat bran
- 1⅓ cups flour
- ½ cup sugar
- ⅛tsp. salt
- 1tsp. baking soda
- 1¼ cups soymilk
- 2tbsp. ground flax seeds
- ½ cup applesauce
- 1tsp. vanilla extract
- ¼ cup sunflower seeds
- ¼ cup raisins

METHOD

1. Preheat your oven to 350°F, and line or grease your muffin tins.
2. Sift together the bran, flour, sugar, baking soda, and salt.
3. Slowly combine with the remaining ingredients.
4. Divide between your muffin cups, then bake for 25 minutes.

Tasty Cornbread

Time: 45mins   **Serves:** 8

INGREDIENTS

- 1/3 cup canola oil
- 2/3 cup maple syrup
- 1 cup whole wheat flour
- 1 cup plain soymilk
- 1 cup fine cornmeal
- 1tsp. salt
- 1tbsp. baking powder

METHOD

1. Preheat your oven to 350°F, and grease a 9x9 square pan.
2. Combine all the ingredients well, then pour into your pan and bake for 35 minutes.

Apple Muffins

Time: 30mins   **Serves:** 12

INGREDIENTS

ingredients

- 2 1/4 cups whole wheat flour
- 1/2tsp. salt
- 1/2 cup brown sugar
- 1tbsp. baking powder
- 2 cups plain soymilk
- 1tsp. cinnamon
- 3tbsp. vegetable oil
- 1 apple, peeled and cut into 1cm cubes
- 1 1/2tsp. vanilla extract

METHOD

1. Preheat your oven to 400°F, and grease your muffin tins.
2. Slowly mix together all the ingredients but the apple, until you get a lumpy batter.
3. Fold in the apple, then pour into your muffin tins, and bake for twenty minutes.

Rosemary and Tomato Scones

Time: 25mins   **Serves:** 12

INGREDIENTS

- 3 cups all-purpose flour
- 1/4 cup sugar
- 2tbsp. baking powder
- 1/2tsp. salt
- 1/3 cup olive oil
- 1/2tsp. pepper
- 14oz. can tomato sauce
- 2tbsp. fresh rosemary, chopped
- 1tsp. apple cider vinegar

METHOD

1. Preheat your oven to 400°F, and grease a large baking sheet.
2. Combine your baking powder, flour, salt, sugar, and pepper.
3. In a separate bowl, mix together everything else.
4. Make a well in the center of the dry ingredients, then add the liquid, and gently combine using a wooden spoon.
5. Being careful not to overmix, turn out onto a floured surface and knead gently until you get a soft dough.
6. Divide into twelve mounds and bake, on your sheet, for 14-16 minutes.
7. Leave to cool on a wire rack, then serve.

Garlic Naan Bread

Time: 2hrs 30mins   **Serves:** 12

INGREDIENTS

- 3½ cups all-purpose flour
- 1tsp. salt
- 1 cup whole wheat flour
- 1tsp. baking powder
- 1½tsp. ground cumin
- 1tsp. ground coriander
- 1 cup plain soymilk
- ¼ cup garlic, finely chopped
- 1 cup vegan sour cream

METHOD

1. Combine your baking powder, flour, salt, cumin, and coriander.
2. Add the soy milk and vegan sour cream, then knead until it holds itself together.
3. Tip onto a floured surface, and knead until smooth and elastic.
4. Pop into a greased bowl covered in a towel, and leave to prove for an hour or so.
5. Divide into twelve balls, then press into round discs.
6. Roll each one to roughly eight inches long, and a quarter-inch thick, then cook on a hot griddle for two to three minutes, or until it puffs and develops blackish brown spots.

Coconut Milk and Banana French Toast

Time: 40mins   **Serves:** 4

INGREDIENTS

- 1 cup coconut milk
- 1 cup rice milk or 1 cup soymilk
- 1tsp. vanilla
- 1 banana
- ¼tsp. cinnamon
- ¼tsp. nutmeg, freshly grated
- 1½tsp. cornstarch
- 8 slices multigrain bread
- ¼tsp. salt

METHOD

1. Chuck everything but the bread into a blender, and process until smooth, then set aside.
2. Heat your griddle and grease well.
3. Dip your bread into the batter, then pop onto the pan.
4. Cook until golden, then flip and cook on the other side.
5. Repeat with each slice.

Pull-Apart Garlic Bread

Time: 15mins   **Serves:** 2

INGREDIENTS

- 3 garlic cloves, minced
- ¼ cup olive oil
- 1 hoagie roll (6-8 inches long), quartered
- dried oregano

METHOD

1. Preheat your oven to 350°F.
2. Lay your bread cut-side-up, and score lengthwise a few times.
3. In a bowl, combine the garlic and olive oil, then microwave for a half-minute.
4. Spoon over the bread, then sprinkle with oregano.
5. Bake for five to ten minutes, until almost dry, then switch to the broiler until the top is browned.

Buttermilk (ish) Biscuits

Time: 30mins   **Serves:** 8-10

INGREDIENTS

- 1tbsp. baking powder
- 2 cups unbleached all-purpose flour
- 1/2 cup Earth Balance whipped spread
- 3/4tsp. salt
- 3/4 cup unsweetened soymilk
- 11/2tsp. lemon juice
- Chives, to serve

METHOD

1. Preheat your oven to 375°F.
2. Stir your lemon juice into the soymilk and leave to rest.
3. Combine all your dry ingredients.
4. Add the Earth Balance, and cut it into the dry mixture with two knives until lumpy or flakey.
5. Stir in the soymilk and combine well until a dough forms.
6. Tip onto a floured surface, then roll into a sausage, and divide into eight pieces.
7. Book for fifteen minutes, or until golden.

Banana Muffins

Time: 45mins   **Serves:** 12

INGREDIENTS

Ingredients

- 11/4 cups whole wheat flour
- 1/2 cup sugar
- 1/4 cup quick oats
- 3tbsp. ground flax seeds
- 1tsp. ground cinnamon
- 1tsp. baking soda
- 1/2tsp. salt
- 1/3 cup unsweetened applesauce
- 1 cup very ripe banana, mashed
- 1/2tsp. vanilla extract
- 3tbsp. mini chocolate chips
- 1/2 cup chopped walnuts

METHOD

1. Preheat your oven to 350°F, and grease your muffin tins.
2. Take two bowls. Combine the dry ingredients in one, then the wet ingredients in another. Combine the two, then fold in the walnuts and chocolate chips.
3. Divide between muffin tins, and bake for 25-30 minutes.

Spiced Carrot Muffins

Time: 20mins   **Serves:** 12

INGREDIENTS

- 13/4 cups whole wheat graham flour
- 1tbsp. ground flax seeds
- 1/4 cup sugar
- 1tsp. baking powder
- 1tsp. ground cinnamon
- 1tsp. baking soda
- 3/4tsp. ginger
- 1/2tsp. salt
- 1/4tsp. pumpkin spice
- 2/3 cup unsweetened applesauce
- 1/4 cup water
- 1/2 cup vanilla soymilk
- 1tsp. vanilla
- 1/2 cup raisins
- 1 cup shredded carrot

METHOD

1. Preheat your oven to 400°F, and grease your muffin pans.
2. Combine all the dry ingredients, then add the wet ingredients and mix well.
3. Fold in the carrots and raisins.   Divide into the muffin cups, then bake for 15 to 20 minutes.

Peanut Butter French Toast

Time: 21mins   **Serves:** 3

INGREDIENTS

- 1tsp. cinnamon
- 1/4 cup peanut butter
- 1/2tsp. vanilla
- 1 cup soymilk
- 2tbsp. flour
- 1/2tsp. oil
- 6 slices bread

METHOD

1. Mix together the cinnamon, soymilk, peanut butter, vanilla, and flour in a medium sized bowl, whisking till smooth.
2. Heat the oil in the pan.
3. Submerge the bread in the batter, and cook until golden brown on each side.

Simple Strawberry Muffins

Time: 25mins   **Serves:** 12

INGREDIENTS

- 3/4 cup whole wheat flour
- 1/4tsp. salt
- 3/4 cup all-purpose flour
- 1/2 cup granulated sugar
- 1tsp. baking powder
- 3/4 cup soymilk
- 1tsp. baking soda
- 1/3 cup canola oil
- 1 cup strawberry (fresh or thawed)
- 1tsp. vanilla extract

METHOD

1. Preheat your oven to 375°F, and grease 12 muffin pans.
2. Combine all the ingredients but the strawberries until mixed but lumpy.
3. Fold in the strawberries, then divide between the pans.
4. Cook for fifteen to twenty minutes.
5. Leave to cool a little in the pan, then turn out onto a wire rack.

Chocolate Chip and Banana Muffins

Time: 35mins

INGREDIENTS

- 2 cups all-purpose flour
- 1 pinch salt
- 1/2 cup vegetable oil
- 1tsp. baking soda
- 1 cup packed brown sugar
- 1 cup unsweetened applesauce
- 1tsp. vanilla extract
- 1/4 cup soymilk
- 3 ripe bananas, mashed
- 1/2 cup walnuts, chopped
- 1 cup vegan chocolate chips

METHOD

1. Preheat your oven to 350°F, and grease your muffin pans.
2. Combine the baking soda, flour, and salt, and reserve.
3. In another bowl, mix all the remaining ingredients, then blend with the flour mixture, being careful not to over mix.
4. Divide between your pans, then cook for 25 to 30 minutes.

Spelt Flour Cornbread

Time: 35mins   **Serves:** 6-8

INGREDIENTS

- 1 cup spelt flour
- 1/4tsp. salt
- 1 cup cornmeal
- 5tsp. baking powder
- 2tbsp. safflower oil (or sunflower oil)
- 1tbsp. maple syrup
- 11/4 cups water

METHOD

1. Preheat your oven to 350°F, and grease a casserole dish.
2. Combine the ingredients, and cook for 22 minutes.

Orange Chocolate Muffins

Time: 35mins

INGREDIENTS

- 1/3 cup sugar
- 23/4 cups whole wheat flour
- 1tsp. baking soda
- 1 orange, juice and zest of
- 2tbsp. cocoa powder
- 1/3 cup chocolate chips
- 1/2-1 cup water or orange juice
- 1/3 cup vegetable oil

METHOD

1. Preheat your oven to 400°F, and grease your muffin pans.
2. Reserve a third of your choc chips, then mix together all the remaining ingredients.
3. Divide between your pans, and cook for fifteen to twenty minutes.

Oatmeal and Peanut Butter Muffins

Time: 30mins   **Serves:** 12-20

INGREDIENTS

- 11/2tsp. baking powder
- 3/4 cup soymilk
- 1 cup oats
- 1 cup flour
- 1 egg substitute
- 1/3 cup maple syrup
- 1/2 cup peanut butter

METHOD

1. Preheat your oven to 400°F, and grease your muffin pans.
2. Combine the flour, baking powder, and oats.
3. Stir in the remaining ingredients, and bake for 20-25 minutes.

Tasty Raisin Bran Muffins

Time: 40mins

INGREDIENTS

- ½ cup oat bran
- ⅓ cup sugar
- 1 cup whole wheat flour
- 1tbsp. baking powder
- 1tsp. salt
- 1tsp. baking soda
- ½ cup raisins
- ½ cup walnuts, chopped
- 1 cup boiling water
- ¼ cup ground flax seeds
- 1 cup natural bran
- ¼ cup soymilk
- 1tbsp. egg substitute
- ¼ cup applesauce
- 1 cup soymilk
- ¼ cup molasses

METHOD

1. Preheat your own to 400°F, and grease your muffin cups.
2. Leave the raisins to soak in the boiling water.
3. Combine the flour, bran, sugar, baking soda, baking powder, salt, walnuts, and flax seeds.
4. Combine the egg replacement with the soymilk, then stir in the apple sauce and molasses.
5. Drain the raisins, reserving the water, then coat in flour.
6. Combine the wet and dry ingredients, then fold in the raisins. Leave stand.
7. Cook for fifteen to twenty minutes.

Tofu French Toast

Time: 25mins   **Serves:** 6

INGREDIENTS

- ½ cup water
- 8oz. silken tofu
- 1tsp. artificial sweetener (molasses or maple syrup)
- 1 banana
- ½tsp. cinnamon
- 6 slices bread
- maple syrup
- fresh berries

METHOD

1. Combine everything but the bread, maple syrup, and berries until smooth.
2. Submerge the bread into this, then cook in a hot pan until golden brown on both sides.
3. Drizzle with syrup, and top with berries to serve.

Pumpkin Scones

Time: 30mins   **Serves:** 12

INGREDIENTS

- 3½ cups flour
- ½tsp. baking soda
- ½ cup sugar
- 2tsp. baking powder
- 3tsp. ginger powder
- 2 cups pumpkin puree
- ½ cup margarine

METHOD

1. Preheat your oven to 425°F.
2. Combine all the dry ingredients, then add the margarine a little at a time.
3. Stir in the pumpkin, and combine.
4. Tip onto a floured surface and knead for a few minutes.
5. Cut into 12 triangular pieces, then cook for twelve to fifteen minutes.

Gluten-Free Banana Bread

Time: 55mins   **Serves:** 12-15

INGREDIENTS

- 1½ cups millet flour
- 1½ cups brown rice flour
- ⅓ cup sugar
- 2tsp. cinnamon
- 3tbsp. ground flax seeds
- 3tsp. baking powder
- ½tsp. salt
- 1tsp. guar gum
- 3 bananas, ripe, mashed
- ⅔ cup walnuts, chopped
- 1½ cups rice milk

METHOD

1. Preheat your oven to 350°F, and grease a loaf pan.
2. Mix together the millet flour, rice flour, sugar, cinnamon, flax seed, baking powder, guar gum, and salt.
3. Add the milk and banana, then mix well.
4. Cook for 45 minutes to an hour, then allow to cool in the pan.

Pumpkin Muffins

Time: 33mins   **Serves:** 12

INGREDIENTS

- 1½ cups sugar
- ¼tsp. salt
- 1tbsp. baking powder
- 1tsp. cinnamon
- ½tsp. ginger
- ½tsp. nutmeg
- ¼tsp. allspice
- 1 cup pumpkin puree
- ⅛tsp. clove, or ½tbsp. pumpkin pie seasoning
- 1¾ cups all-purpose flour
- ½ cup soymilk
- 2tbsp. molasses
- ½ cup vegetable oil

METHOD

1. Preheat your oven to 400°F, and grease 12 muffin pans.
2. Mix together the salt, flour, baking powder, and spices.
3. In another bowl, combine the soy milk, pumpkin, vegetable oil, and molasses.
4. Combine the two mixes, then divide between your muffin pans.
5. Cook for eighteen to twenty minutes.

Spelt Rolls

Time: 43mins   **Serves:** 15

INGREDIENTS

- 1 cup warm water
- 2tbsp. dry yeast
- ⅓ cup refined coconut oil, melted
- ¼ cup coconut sugar
- 1tbsp. flax seed meal
- 3tbsp. water
- 1½tsp. salt
- 1tsp. poppy or sesame seeds
- 3½ cups spelt flour

METHOD

1. Preheat your oven to 400°F, and grease a 9"x13" pan.
2. Combine the flaxseed meal with 3 tbsp water, then allow it to rest for fifteen minutes, until the water is absorbed and the mixture is gloopy.
3. Mix together the coconut oil, water, yeast, and sugar, and leave to rest for fifteen minutes.
4. Attach your dough hook to your mixer, then add the salt, flaxseed mix, the yeast mix, and the floor.
5. Knead the dough with the hook until smooth and soft.
6. Divide into twelve rolls, and leave to rest on your greased pan for ten minutes.
7. Cook for eighteen minutes.   Brush with melted vegan butter, then sprinkle the seeds on and leave to cool.

Apple and Cinnamon Muffins

Time: 25mins

INGREDIENTS

- ¼tsp. cinnamon
- ¾ cup whole wheat flour
- 1 cup all-purpose flour
- ½ cup ground flax seeds
- 1½tbsp. baking powder
- ½ cup granulated sugar
- 1tsp. cinnamon
- 1 apple, finely chopped with skin on
- 2tbsp. granulated sugar
- ¼tsp. salt
- 1 cup water
- 111g. unsweetened applesauce
- ¼ cup olive oil

METHOD

1. Preheat your oven to 400°F, and grease a muffin pan.
2. Mix the quarter teaspoons of cinnamon and sugar, and sprinkle around your muffin pan.
3. Combine the dry ingredients, then add the wet ingredients and mix until combined but still lumpy.
4. Fold in the apples. Bake for fifteen minutes, or until cooked through.

Strawberry and Chocolate Muffins

Time: 35mins   **Serves:** 12

INGREDIENTS

- ⅓ cup cocoa powder
- 1½ cups all-purpose flour
- ¾ cup sugar
- ¼ cup margarine
- 1tsp. baking powder
- 2 Ener-G Egg Substitute
- ¼ cup vegetable oil
- 2tsp. vanilla extract
- ¾ cup soymilk
- 12 strawberries
- 1 cup Ghirardelli semi-sweet chocolate chips

METHOD

1. Preheat your oven to 350°F, and grease 12 muffin tins.
2. Mix together the sugar, cocoa powder, flour, and baking powder. Melt the margarine with a quarter of the chocolate chips carefully in the microwave, then leave to cool slightly.
3. Beat the egg replacement with the oil, vanilla, and soymilk, then stir in the margarine/chocolate mix.
4. Sift in the dry ingredients, and mix, then stir in a half-cup of chocolate chips.
5. Divide between the muffin tins, then push a strawberry into the center of each one. Add a little more batter to ensure the fruit is fully covered.
6. Sprinkle with the remaining chocolate chips, then bake for 25 minutes.
7. Leave to cool in the tin, then turn out onto a wire rack.

Apple and Gingerbread Muffins

Time: 35mins   **Serves:** 12

INGREDIENTS

GINGERBREAD BATTER

- 1 ¼ cups all-purpose flour
- 1tsp. baking soda
- ⅓ cup brown sugar
- ½tsp. ground cloves
- ½tsp. ground cinnamon
- ½tsp. ground ginger
- 1 Ener-G Egg Substitute
- ⅓ cup molasses
- 3tbsp. margarine, melted
- ½ cup hot water

APPLE BOTTOMS

- 2 large apples, peeled, cored, and cut into 1-inch cubes.
- 2tbsp. brown sugar
- 1tbsp. margarine, melted

METHOD

1. Preheat your oven to 350°F.
2. Coat your apple chunks in the margarine and brown sugar, then spoon into the bottoms of a muffin pan. Mix together the brown sugar, flour, baking soda, and spices.
3. In another bowl, combine the egg replacement, molasses, melted margarine, and hot water, then mix this into your sugar and flour mixture. Spoon over the apples, and bake for 25 minutes.

Pumpkin Bread

Time: 1hr 5mins   **Serves:** 20

INGREDIENTS

- ½ cup water
- ½ cup applesauce
- 1½ cups turbinado sugar
- ½ cup canola oil
- 3 cups whole wheat flour
- 2 cups pumpkin puree
- 3tbsp. ground flax seed
- 1tsp. cinnamon
- 1tsp. ground ginger
- 1tsp. fresh nutmeg
- 1tsp. baking soda
- ¾tsp. salt
- ½tsp. baking powder
- 1 cup walnuts, chopped

METHOD

1. Preheat your oven to 350°F, and grease two 8-inch loaf pans.
2. Combine the flaxseed and water until thickened and gloopy.
3. Stir in the applesauce, sugar, oil, and pumpkin. In another bowl, combine the spices, flour, baking soda, baking powder, and salt, the combine this with the first mixture.
4. Fold in the walnuts.   Bake for 55 minutes, then let rest for 20 minutes in the pan before serving.

Blueberry Muffins

Time: 35mins   **Serves:** 12

INGREDIENTS

- ½ cup whole wheat flour
- ½ cup unbleached flour
- ½ cup teff flour
- 2tsp. baking powder
- ¾ cup turbinado sugar
- ½tsp. salt
- 1tbsp. Ener-G Egg Substitute
- ⅓ cup canola oil
- ⅓ cup soymilk
- ½tsp. cinnamon
- 1 cup blueberries (fresh or frozen)

CRUMB TOPPING

- ⅛ cup unbleached flour
- ¾tsp. cinnamon
- ¼ cup turbinado sugar
- 2tbsp. vegan margarine

METHOD

1. Preheat your oven to 400°F and grease 12 muffin cups.
2. Combine the flours, sugar, salt, and baking powder.
3. Make the "egg," then add the oil. Add enough soymilk to make it up to a cup of liquid.
4. Combine this with the dry ingredients, then fold in the blueberries.   Divide between the muffin cups.
5. To make the topping, crumb the ingredients together with your fingers, making a thick crumble. Sprinkle over the batter in your cups.   Cook for 25 minutes.

Poppy Seed and Lemon Muffins

Time: 35mins   **Serves:** 12-15

INGREDIENTS

- ½ cup barley flour
- 2tsp. baking powder
- ¼ cup poppy seeds
- 1tsp. baking soda
- 1 cup water
- 2tbsp. flax seeds
- ½ cup frozen apple juice concentrate, thawed
- 2 cups whole wheat pastry flour
- ¼ cup canola oil
- ⅓ cup fresh lemon juice
- ⅓ cup pure maple syrup
- 1tsp. vanilla extract
- 2tbsp. lemon zest

METHOD

1. Mix together the poppy seeds, flours, baking powder, and soda.
2. Grind your flax seeds to a powder in your blender, then add a half-cup of water and blend until gummy.
3. Add the rest of the wet ingredients bar the zest, and blend until frothy.
4. Fold in the zest, then pour into the dry ingredients and stir gently.
5. Divide between muffin cups, then back for twenty minutes.

Zucchini and Chocolate Mini Muffins

Time: 27mins   **Serves:** 36

INGREDIENTS

- 3tbsp. warm water
- ¼ cup unsweetened cocoa
- 1¼ cups whole wheat flour
- 1¼tsp. baking powder
- ½tsp. salt
- ¾tsp. baking soda
- 1tsp. cinnamon
- ½ cup unsweetened applesauce
- 1tbsp. ground flax seeds
- 1 cup sugar
- ¼ cup almond milk
- 1 cup zucchini, shredded
- 1tsp. vanilla extract

METHOD

1. Preheat your oven to 350°F, and grease your mini muffin pan.
2. Combine the ground flax seed with the water and set to the side.
3. Combine the cocoa, flour, baking powder, salt, baking soda, and cinnamon.
4. In another bowl, cream your flax seed mixture with the applesauce and sugar.
5. Stir in the vanilla, almond milk, and shredded zucchini, and combine.
6. Add this to the dry mix, and combine well.
7. Divide between your mini muffin cups, and bake for 12-15 minutes.

Chickpea Crackers

Time: 20mins   **Serves:** 20

INGREDIENTS

- 2 cups chickpea flour
- 1tsp. baking powder
- 4tbsp. toasted sesame seeds (lightly ground in food processor or mortar)
- 4tbsp. nutritional yeast
- 4tbsp. toasted sesame seeds (whole)
- 1tsp. salt
- ½tsp. turmeric
- ¾-1 cup water
- 1tsp. sesame oil

METHOD

1. Preheat your oven to 350°F, and grease a cookie sheet.
2. Combine your dry ingredients, then stir in the sesame oil.
3. Slowly add the water until a dough forms a ball.
4. Tip onto a floured surface, roll out, and cut into circles.
5. Pop onto your cookie sheet and prick with a fork.
6. Bake for 15-20 minutes, or until they're crisp in the center.

Cornbread

Time: 40mins   **Serves:** 6

INGREDIENTS

- 1 cup flour
- 1 cup cornmeal
- 5tsp. baking powder
- 2tbsp. sunflower oil
- ¼tsp. salt
- 1¼ cups water
- 1tsp. poppy seed
- 2tbsp. blackstrap molasses

METHOD

1. Preheat your oven to 400°F, and oil a 10-inch pie plate.
2. Mix together all the wet ingredients, then all the dry ingredients, and then combine the two mixtures until smooth.
3. Pour into your pie plate, and sprinkle with poppy seeds. Bake for twenty minutes.

Simple Good-For-You Muffins

Time: 30mins   **Serves:** 12

INGREDIENTS

- 1 cup whole wheat flour
- 1 cup all-purpose flour
- 1/4 cup soy flour
- 1tbsp. baking powder
- 1/4tsp. ground nutmeg
- 1/2tsp. ground cinnamon
- 1/4tsp. ground allspice
- 1/2 cup sugar
- 1/2tsp. salt
- 1/2 cup raisins
- 1/4 cup molasses
- 2tbsp. ground flax seeds
- 1/2 cup applesauce
- 1/4 cup vegetable oil
- 1 cup soymilk

METHOD

1. Preheat your oven to 375°F, and grease a twelve cup muffin tin.
2. Mix together the baking powder, flours, cinnamon, allspice, nutmeg, salt, raisins, sugar, and flax seeds.
3. In another bowl, beat the molasses with the applesauce, soymilk, and oil.
4. Combine the two mixtures, then divide between the muffin cups.   Bake for 20-25 minutes.

Almond Mocha Muffins

Time: 30mins   **Serves:** 10-12

INGREDIENTS

- 6tbsp. unsweetened cocoa powder
- 1/2tsp. baking soda
- 1tsp. baking powder
- 1/4tsp. salt
- 1/3 cup rice syrup
- 3/4 cup strong coffee, lukewarm
- 11/2 cups whole wheat pastry flour
- 1/4 cup canola oil
- 11/2tsp. almond extract
- 1tbsp. rice wine vinegar
- 1/2 cup non-dairy chocolate chips
- powdered sugar
- 1/2 cup slivered almonds

METHOD

1. Preheat your oven to 325°F, and grease a muffin tin.
2. Combine your cocoa, flour, baking powder, baking soda, and salt.
3. In another bowl, combine the syrup, coffee, oil, vinegar, and almond extract.
4. Blend these two mixes together, then fold in the chocolate chips.
5. Divide between your muffin cups, and top with almonds.
6. Bake for twenty minutes, then leave to cool for ten minutes before removing from the tin and sprinkling with powdered sugar.

Simple Blueberry Muffins

Time: 30mins   **Serves:** 3-4

INGREDIENTS

- 3/4 cup whole wheat flour
- 1tsp. baking soda
- 2tsp. baking powder
- 5tbsp. sugar
- 1/4 cup vegetable oil
- 3/4 cup soy milk
- 1tbsp. ground flax seed
- 1 1/4 cups all-purpose flour
- 1 cup blueberries
- 3tbsp. water

METHOD

1. Preheat your over to 375°F, and grease a muffin pan.
2. Mix your ground flax seed with three tablespoons of water, then leave to absorb.
3. Combine all the dry ingredients, combine all the wet ingredients including the flaxseed mix, then combine the two mixtures well.
4. Fold in the blueberries.   Divide between your muffin cups, and cook for twenty minutes.

Easy Pumpkin Bread

Time: 1hr 20mins

INGREDIENTS

- 15oz. can pumpkin
- 3 cups sugar
- ½ cup oil
- 3½ cups flour
- ½ cup unsweetened applesauce
- 3tbsp. flax seeds
- 1tsp. baking powder
- ½ cup water
- 1tsp. baking soda
- ¼tsp. ground cloves
- ½tsp. salt
- ½tsp. allspice
- 1tsp. cinnamon
- ½tsp. nutmeg

METHOD

1. Preheat your oven to 350°F.
2. Grind your flax seeds, then mix with the water until well-blended and fully absorbed.
3. Combine your pumpkin, water, sugar, oil, and applesauce.
4. Sift the dry ingredients together, then pour in the pumpkin and fold to combine.
5. Bake for an hour.

Carrot and Cinnamon Mini Muffins

Time: 1hr   **Serves:** 12

INGREDIENTS

- ¾tsp. baking powder
- ⅜ cup sugar
- ¼ cup unsweetened applesauce
- 1¼ cups all-purpose flour
- ¾tsp. cinnamon
- 1tsp. baking soda
- ¼tsp. nutmeg
- ⅛ cup grapeseed oil
- ¼tsp. salt
- 1tbsp. honey
- ½ cup water
- 1 cup carrot, grated

METHOD

1. Preheat your oven to 325°F.
2. Stir your baking powder into the applesauce, then reserve.
3. Combine your flour, nutmeg, baking soda, sugar, cinnamon, and salt.
4. Stir in the carrots, honey, water, and applesauce mixture, and combine.
5. Divide into cupcake liners, and bake for thirty minutes.

Apple and Raisin Wheat Bran Muffins

Time: 28mins   **Serves:** 16

INGREDIENTS

- 14oz. tofu
- 1 apple, unpeeled, cored, quartered
- ½ cup soymilk
- ¾ cup Splenda sugar substitute
- 2tsp. vanilla extract
- ¾tsp. salt
- 1tsp. cinnamon
- 2tsp. baking powder
- 1 cup white whole wheat flour
- ½ cup raisins
- 2½ cups wheat bran

METHOD

1. Preheat your oven to 350°F.
2. Pulse everything but the raisins in a food processor until combined, then fold in the raisins.
3. Using an ice cream scoop, for 16 muffins on a tray.
4. Bake for 23 minutes.

Garlic Bread

Time: 2hrs 30mins   **Serves:** 4-8

INGREDIENTS

- 3/4 cup plus 2tbsp. water
- 2 1/2 cups all-purpose flour
- 1tsp. dry active yeast
- 1/2 tsp. salt
- 4tbsp. extra virgin olive oil
- 3 garlic cloves, finely minced
- 1tbsp. vegan butter
- 1 pinch salt
- handful parsley, roughly chopped

METHOD

1. Stir the yeast into the water, and leave to rest for ten minutes, until activated.
2. Add the flour and salt, and combine.
3. Coat the dough in a little oil, then cover with a damp tea towel, and leave to prove for two to three hours, or until doubled in size.   Preheat your oven 350°F, and grease a baking tray with olive oil.
4. Push the dough down, then tip onto your baking tray and spread into an oval shape with your fingers, until a half-inch thick. Cover again with a damp tea towel, and leave for another thirty minutes.
5. Score the dough, then back for 25 to 30 minutes.   Meanwhile, heat the olive oil, vegan butter, and garlic until melted and combined. Remove from the heat, stir in the parsley, and pour over your freshly cooked bread.

Sticky Buns

Time: 3hrs 25mins   **Serves:** 12

INGREDIENTS

PASTE

- 1/3 cup water
- 1/4 cup all-purpose flour

DOUGH

- 2tsp. dry active yeast
- 4 cups and 2tbsp. all-purpose flour
- 1 cup lukewarm water
- 1/4 cup granulated sugar
- 1/4 cup vegetable oil
- 1tsp. salt

FILLING AND TOPPING

- 1/2 cup vegan butter
- 3tbsp. maple syrup
- 1 cup light brown sugar
- 1 cup walnut halves, roughly chopped
- 1tbsp. all-purpose flour
- 1tbsp. ground cinnamon

METHOD

1. Make the paste but mixing the ingredients together, then heating over a medium flame until thickened into a paste. Remove from the heat, and leave to cool.   Make the dough by combining the yeast and lukewarm water, then leave it rest for ten minutes, or until active.
2. Add the cooled paste, then the sugar, flour, salt, and vegetable oil.
3. Using the dough hook in your mix, knead the dough for six minutes on a medium spped.
4. Coat the dough in a little oil, then cover with a damp tea towel and leave to prove for around two hours, or until doubled in size.   Make the topping by creaming the butter with the sugar.
5. Take out a third of this mixture, and reserve the rest. In the third, stir in the maple syrup until smooth, then add the walnuts. Preheat your oven to 350°F.
6. Dot the walnut mixture over a deep, 9x13-inch baking pan. Pop it into the oven and cook until melted.
7. Remove from the oven, and spread evenly over the base of the pan.
8. To the remaining butter-sugar mixture, stir in the cinnamon and flour.
9. Shape your dough into a 18x12-inch rectangle, and spread the sugar mix all over the surface.
10. Roll into a log, then cut into twelve pieces and place cut-side down on the baking tray.
11. Cover again, and leave to prove for another thirty to forty minutes.   Uncover and bake for 25-30 minutes. Remove from the tray while still hot, then allow to cool before serving.

Kefir, Coconut, and Banana Muffins

Time: 45mins   **Serves:** 12

INGREDIENTS

- 1 cup granulated sugar
- 2tsp. baking soda
- 1 cup unsweetened dried shredded coconut
- 1tsp. baking powder
- 2 ripe bananas, mashed
- 2 cups all-purpose flour
- ½tsp. salt
- 1½ cups pc dairy-free kefir probiotic fermented
- coconut milk
- 1tsp. vanilla extract
- ¼ cup cold-pressed liquid coconut oil

METHOD

1. 1. Preheat your oven to 350°F, and grease a 12 cup muffin tin.
2. 2. Combine your sugar, flour, coconut, baking powder, baking soda, and salt.
3. 3. In another bowl, combine the kefir, bananas, coconut oil, and vanilla.
4. Add to flour mixture and stir until combined.
5. Divide between the muffin cups, and bake for thirty minutes.
6. Allow to cool in the tin for fifteen minutes.

Banana Bread with Chocolate Chips

Time: 1hr   **Serves:** 10

INGREDIENTS

- 1tsp. Ener-G Egg Substitute
- 1tsp. baking powder
- 75g. demerara sugar
- 75g. olive oil
- 25g. granulated sugar
- 225g. self-raising flour
- 1tsp. apple cider vinegar
- 75g dark chocolate chips
- 4 ripe bananas, mashed

METHOD

1. Preheat your oven to 175°C, and grease a loaf tin.
2. Combine all the dry ingredients.
3. Stir in the vinegar, oil, and then the bananas. Fold in the chocolate chips.
4. Cook for 45-50mins.

Sweet Potato Biscuits

Time: 22mins   **Serves:** 9

INGREDIENTS

- ¾ cup mashed sweet potato
- ⅓ cup soymilk
- 1tsp. apple cider vinegar
- 1½ cups whole wheat pastry flour
- 2tbsp. sugar
- 1tbsp. baking powder
- ½-1tsp. salt
- 5tbsp. cold Earth Balance butter or coconut oil
- 8oz. vegan honey

METHOD

1. Preheat your oven to 425°F, and line a baking sheet with parchment paper.
2. Combine the vinegar, sweet potato, and non-dairy milk.
3. Combine the sugar, flour, baking powder, and salt in a food processor, and pulse.
4. Add the oil or butter, and pulse to create a coarse meal.
5. Add the sweet potato mixture, and pulse a little more.
6. Tip onto a floured surface, then fold over a couple of times, and pat down to a half-inch thick.
7. Using a cookie cutter, cut into biscuits, then pop onto your sheet.
8. Bake for twelve minutes, then serve immediately.

Nutty Chocolate 'Butter' Muffins

Time: 28mins   **Serves:** 6

INGREDIENTS

- 1/4tsp. baking powder
- 3/4 cup multigrain flour
- 1/4tsp. baking soda
- 2tbsp. nut butter
- 2tbsp. cocoa powder
- 1tbsp. flourless oil
- 1/2-3/4 cup almond milk
- 2tbsp. liquid sweetener (Maple Syrup, Agave)

METHOD

1. Preheat your oven to 350°F, and grease a muffin tin. Combine the sweetener, oil, milk, and nut-butter.
2. In another bowl, mix together the baking soda, flour, baking powder, cocoa powder, and salt.
3. Combine the two mixtures well. Divide the batter between the muffin cups, and bake for 15-18 minutes.

Biscuits with White Country Gravy

Time: 50mins   **Serves:** 4

INGREDIENTS

- 2tbsp. baking powder
- 1qt. all-purpose flour, plus extra for dusting
- 2tsp. salt
- 2 cups soymilk
- 3/4 cup margarine
- 1tbsp. canola oil
- 3tbsp. garlic, minced
- 1½tbsp. flour
- 1tbsp. gravy seasoning
- 6tbsp. cooked vegan sausage, 1/8-inch diced
- 2 cups unsweetened soymilk

METHOD

1. Sift together the dry ingredients, then rub the margarine in with your hands.
2. Add the soymilk, and again combine using your hands. Pop in the fridge for an hour.
3. Preheat your oven to 400°F.   Tip onto a floured surface, flatten the dough, and flour the top. Cut into biscuits.   Bake for 25 minutes.   Meanwhile, sauté the sausage for five minutes.
4. Heat the oil over a medium-high heat, then stir in the garlic and seasoning mix. Add the flour and whisk to form a roux. Whisk in the soymilk, then cook over low-medium heat until the gravy thickens.

Chocolate Chip and Pecan Pumpkin Bread

Time: 1hr 30mins   **Serves:** 36

INGREDIENTS

- 4 cups unbleached all-purpose flour
- 1tsp. salt
- 2tsp. baking soda
- 1tsp. ground cinnamon
- 2 cups coconut sugar crystals
- 1/2tsp. nutmeg
- 3/4 cup vegan butter
- 5tbsp. flax seeds
- 12½ water
- 1/2 cup water
- 1 cup vegan semi-sweet
- chocolate chips
- 15oz. can pumpkin puree
- 2tbsp. pecans, chopped
- 2tbsp. vegan semi-sweet chocolate chips
- 2tbsp. coconut sugar crystals

METHOD

1. Stir the flaxseed into the water, and leave to thicken for fifteen minutes.
2. Preheat your oven to 350°F, and grease 2 9X5 inch loaf pans.
3. Combine the baking soda, flour, salt, nutmeg, cinnamon.
4. In your stand mixer, combine the sugar and butter on medium speed, until creamy. Add the flax egg a bit at a time, then add the water and pumpkin on a low speed.
5. Add the flour mixture a cup at a time, then continue beating for another minutes.
6. Add the chocolate chips, coconut sugar, and pecans, then pour into the loaf pans and bake for 1 hour 5 minutes.   Cool in the pan for ten minutes, then tip onto a wire rack.

Chunky Chocolate Muffins

Time: 43mins   **Serves:** 6

INGREDIENTS

- ¼ cup unsweetened applesauce
- 1 cup soymilk
- ¼ cup canola oil
- 2 cups whole wheat flour
- 1tsp. vanilla extract
- ½ cup white sugar
- ½cup of vegan dark chocolate bar, chopped
- ½tbsp. baking soda

METHOD

1. Preheat your oven to 350°F, and grease a muffin tin.
2. Combine all the dry ingredients, then mix in the milk, oil, applesauce, and vanilla extract.
3. Fold in the chocolate, then divide between the muffin cups.   Bake for 23 minutes.

Gluten-Free Garlic Breadsticks

Time: 2hrs 25mins   **Serves:** 18

INGREDIENTS

DOUGH

- 1tsp. sugar
- 2tbsp. ground flax seeds
- ½ cup warm water
- 500g. gluten-free flour
- 1tsp. guar gum
- 2tsp. garlic powder
- 4tsp. dry active yeast
- ¼ cup extra-virgin olive oil
- warm water
- 1½tsp. salt

BREADSTICKS

- ¼ cup olive oil
- ¼tsp. dried oregano
- 3 garlic cloves, minced
- ¼tsp. dried basil
- 1 pinch ground pepper
- ¼tsp. dried parsley

METHOD

1. To make the dough, mix together the sugar, yeast, and warm water, then leave to activate for ten minutes.
2. Mix your flour, flaxseed, garlic powder, and guar gum, then stir in the yeast mixture, and stir together for three minutes.
3. Stir in the salt and oil, and mix to form a soft dough.   Set aside, and leave to prove for an hour.
4. Knock it back, knead again for a few minutes, then let it rest for another five minutes.
1. Preheat your oven to 375°F. Combine the oil, garlic, and herbs.
2. Shape your dough into eighteen breadsticks, then pop onto your parchment paper, brush with garlic oil, and let rise for thirty minutes.
3. Bake for twenty minutes.

Fat-Free Biscuits

Time: 20mins   **Serves:** 2

INGREDIENTS

- ½tsp. baking soda
- 1 cup oat flour
- ½ cup unsweetened applesauce
- ⅛tsp. salt

METHOD

1. Preheat your oven to 400°F, and grease a cookie sheet.
2. Combine your dry ingredients, then add the applesauce.
3. Shape into six biscuits, and transfer to the sheet.
4. Bake for eight to ten minutes, until lightly brown.

Sweet Cornbread

Time: 40mins   **Serves:** 9

INGREDIENTS

- 1 cup whole wheat pastry flour
- 1tsp. salt
- 2/3 cup unrefined sugar
- 2½tsp. baking powder
- 1/3 cup extra light olive oil
- 1 cup cornmeal
- ½tsp. baking soda
- ½ cup almond milk
- 1-2tbsp. cinnamon sugar
- ½ cup water

METHOD

1. Preheat your oven to 350°F, and grease an 8x8" baking dish.
2. Combine your dry ingredients, then add the wet ingredients and stir gently.
3. Pour into the dish, and sprinkle with cinnamon sugar.
4. Bake for thirty minutes. Cool for fifteen minutes before serving.

Pineapple and Zucchini Muffins

Time: 55mins

INGREDIENTS

- 2 cups unbleached white flour
- 1tbsp. baking powder
- 3/4 cup sugar
- 1tbsp. baking soda
- ½tbsp. ground ginger
- 1tbsp. cinnamon
- 1½tsp. salt
- 2½ cups whole wheat flour
- 2 cups applesauce
- 1 cup shredded coconut
- 20oz. can crushed
- pineapple, drained
- 3 cups shredded zucchini
- 1¼ cups bananas, mashed
- ½tbsp. vanilla extract
- 3/4 cup golden raisins
- 3/4 cup walnuts, chopped

METHOD

1. Preheat your oven to 325°F, and grease a muffin pan.
2. Mix together the sugar, flour, soda, baking powder, cinnamon, ginger, and salt.
3. In another bowl, combine the applesauce, banana, pineapple, and vanilla extract.
4. Combine the two mixtures, then add the walnuts, zucchini, raisins, and coconut.
5. Bake for 25 minutes.

Herbed Crackers

Time: 19mins   **Serves:** 4-6

INGREDIENTS

- 2 cups blanched almond flour
- 2tbsp. Herbes de Provence
- 3/4tsp. salt
- 2tbsp. water
- 1tbsp. olive oil

METHOD

1. Preheat your oven to 350°F.
2. Mix your almond flour with the salt and and Herbes de Provence.
3. Combine your olive oil and water.
4. Stir together the two mixtures, then roll into a ball and press between two sheets of parchment until it's a half-inch thick.
5. Transfer to a baking sheet, removing the paper.
6. Cut dough into 2-inch squares, and bake for around ten minutes.

Nutty Banana and Date Muffins

Time: 30mins   **Serves:** 12

INGREDIENTS

- 2tsp. baking powder
- ½tsp. cinnamon
- ½tsp. baking soda
- ⅛tsp. salt
- 1¼ cups white
- whole-wheat flour
- ½ cup soymilk
- 2 medium ripe bananas
- ¼ cup oil
- 2tbsp. maple syrup
- 2tbsp. molasses
- 1 cup uncooked oats
- ½ cup nuts, chopped
- 1 cup dates, chopped

METHOD

1. Preheat your oven to 375°F, and grease a muffin pan.
2. Mix together your baking powder, flour, baking soda, cinnamon, and salt.
3. Combine the banana, oil, milk, molasses, and maple syrup, then stir in the oatmeal and let it rest for two minutes.   Combine the two mixtures, then fold in the dates and nuts.
4. Divide between your muffin cups, then bake for around sixteen minutes.
5. Cook in the pan for fifteen minutes, then tip out onto a wire cooling rack.

Strawberry and Raspberry Muffins

Time: 1hr   **Serves:** 14

INGREDIENTS

- ½tsp. salt
- ½ cup sugar
- 3tsp. baking powder
- 1 banana, soft
- ¾ cup rice milk
- 2 cups flour
- ¼ cup oil
- 1tsp. vinegar
- ½ cup fresh strawberries, chopped
- 1 cup fresh raspberry

METHOD

1. Preheat your oven to 350°F.
2. Combine your flour with the salt and baking powder.   Combine the rice milk and the vinegar.
3. Combine the two mixtures, then add the remaining ingredients.
4. Divide between muffin cups, and bake for 35-45 minutes.

Orange and Cranberry Scones

Time: 30mins   **Serves:** 24

INGREDIENTS

- ½ cup maple syrup
- 6tbsp. canola oil
- 1 cup orange juice with pulp
- 4tsp. baking powder
- 3 cups white whole wheat flour
- 2tsp. cinnamon
- ½tsp. salt
- ½tsp. ground cloves
- ⅔-1 cup dried cranberries
- 1tbsp. turbinado sugar
- ⅔ cup walnuts, chopped

METHOD

1. Preheat your oven to 375°F, and line a cookie sheet with parchment paper.
2. Combine your oil, syrup, and orange juice.
3. In another bowl, mix the baking powder, flour, spices, and salt.
4. Combine the two mixtures, then fold in the cranberries and walnuts.
5. Tip onto a floured surface, then knead for a few minutes.
6. Shape into three 4-5 inch circles of around an inch thick.
7. Sprinkle with turbinado raw cane sugar, then place on your lined cookie sheet.. Bake for 15-20 minutes

Lemon and Banana Muffins

Time: 35mins   **Serves:** 6

INGREDIENTS

- ½ cup raw sugar
- ½ medium banana
- 2tsp. baking powder
- ¾ cup soymilk
- 4tsp. light oil
- 1⅔ cups flour
- 1tsp. lemon extract

METHOD

1. Preheat your oven to 325°F, and grease a muffin pan.
2. Sift together your sugar, flour, baking supplement, and baking powder.
3. In another bowl, combine the soy milk, banana, lemon extract, and oil.
4. Add the sifted flour mix, and stir until blended.
5. Divide between your muffin cups, and bake for fifteen minutes.

Boston Creme Muffins

Time: 25mins   **Serves:** 12

INGREDIENTS

- 31/2oz. box instant vanilla pudding
- 11/4oz. cups cold non-dairy milk substitute
- 1tbsp. pure vanilla extract
- chocolate icing
- 12 vanilla cupcakes

METHOD

1. Combine your pudding mix, milk, and vanilla, and beat in your mixer for two minutes.
2. Refrigerate for fifteen minutes, then spoon into a piping bag with a medium sized plain tip.
3. Push the tip into the center of each cupcake, and fill.
4. Frost with the chocolate icing, and refrigerate until set.

Simple Pumpkin Muffins

Time: 37mins

INGREDIENTS

- 1¾ cups flour
- 1tbsp. baking powder
- 1tsp. cinnamon
- ¼tsp. salt
- ½tsp. nutmeg
- ¼tsp. allspice
- ½tsp. ginger
- ⅛tsp. ground cloves
- 1tbsp. soy yogurt
- 1¼ cups sugar
- 1 cup pumpkin puree
- ½ cup soymilk
- 2tbsp. molasses
- ½ cup vegetable oil

METHOD

1. Preheat your oven to 400°F, and grease a muffin pan.
2. Sift together all your dry ingredients, then whisk together your wet ingredients in another bowl.
3. Pour the wet into dry, and mix well.
4. Bake for 27-30 minutes.

Pumpkin and Cranberry Bread

Time: 55mins

INGREDIENTS

- 1½ cups white flour
- 3⁄8tsp. salt
- ¼ cup cornmeal
- ¾ cup granulated sugar
- 2 cups whole raw cranberries
- 1tsp. baking soda
- ½tsp. ground cinnamon
- ¼tsp. baking powder
- ½tsp. ground ginger
- 1 cup canned pumpkin puree
- ¼tsp. ground cloves
- 5tbsp. expeller-pressed canola oil
- 3tbsp. water
- 2tsp. grated orange zest

METHOD

1. Preheat your oven to 350°F, and grease a 9-inch cake pan.
2. In your food processor, pulse the cranberries until quartered. Reserve.
3. Pop all your dry ingredients into the processor, and pulse to blend.
4. In a bowl, combine the rest of the ingredients.
5. Add the dry ingredients and chopped cranberries to your wet ingredients, and stir gently.
6. Bake until the bread has shrunk away from the sides of the pan. This should take around 45 minutes.
7. Leave to cool in the pan for ten minutes, then tip onto a wire cooling rack.

Chocolate Apple Bread

Time: 1hr   **Serves:** 15-30

INGREDIENTS

- 12⁄3 cups flour
- 1⁄3 cup cocoa powder
- 1 cup sugar

GLAZE

- 3-4tsp. soymilk
- 1tsp. baking powder
- 1tsp. salt
- 1tsp. baking soda
- 1tsp. cinnamon
- 2 egg substitute
- 1½ cups applesauce
- ½ cup powdered sugar

METHOD

1. Preheat your oven to 350°F, and grease a loaf pan.
2. Gently combine all the ingredients.
3. Bake for fifty minutes, then let cool a little before turning it out of the pan.
4. For the glaze, combine the powdered sugar and soy milk, and drizzle over the top.

Pineapple Muffins

Time: 35mins

INGREDIENTS

- 2tsp. baking powder
- 2 cups unbleached flour
- 2 cups crushed pineapple
- 1 cup sugar
- ½-1 cup soy margarine
- 1tsp. vanilla extract
- ½ cup vanilla-flavored soymilk

METHOD

1. Preheat your oven to 375°F.
2. Sift together your flour, baking powder, and sugar, then stir in the pineapple.
3. Combine the vanilla, soymilk, and soy margarine, then add this to your dry ingredients.
4. Divide between your muffin cups, and bake for 25 minutes.

Beer Bread

Time: 1hr 5mins   **Serves:** 10

INGREDIENTS

- 1tbsp. baking powder
- 2½ cups all-purpose flour
- 2tsp. salt
- ⅓ cup olive oil
- 2tbsp. sugar
- 355ml. brown beer
- 2tsp. melted margarine
- 2tbsp. oatmeal or dried onion
- Sesame seeds

METHOD

Preheat your oven to 350°F, and grease a loaf pan.

1. Combine all the dry ingredients, then slowly add the margarine and the beer.
2. Pour into your loaf pan, then top with margarine and sprinkle with sesame seeds.
3. Bake for fifty minutes.

Cranberry Scones

Time: 37mins

INGREDIENTS

- 4-5tbsp. sugar
- ¾tsp. salt
- 1tbsp. baking powder
- 6tbsp. cold margarine, cut
- into pieces
- 1tsp. orange zest
- 1 cup dried cranberries
- 2 cups all-purpose flour
- ⅓ cup soymilk, plus more for brushing tops
- sugar, for sprinkling
- ½ cup blended extra-firm silken tofu

METHOD

1. Preheat your oven to 400°F.   Sift together the sugar, flour, baking powder, and salt.
2. Cut in the margarine until the pieces are pea-sized.   Stir in the cranberries and orange zest.
3. Beat your soymilk with the tofu, and mix into the dry ingredients.
4. Turn onto a floured surface, and knead for a few minutes.
5. Pat the dough into a 6-inch square, about an inch thick, then quarter. Cut diagonally to form triangles, and pop onto your baking sheet.
6. Brush with soymilk, and top with sugar.   Bake for 20 to 22 minutes.

Graham Crackers

Time: 37mins   **Serves:** 7

INGREDIENTS

- 1½ cups whole wheat pastry flour
- ¼tsp. baking soda
- ½ cup sugar, ground in a
- blender until powdered
- ½tsp. cinnamon
- ¼ cup neutral tasting vegetable oil
- ¼tsp. salt
- 3tbsp. maple syrup
- 2-4tbsp. water, as needed
- 2½tsp. vanilla extract

METHOD

1. Preheat your oven to 350°F, and line a baking sheet with parchment paper.
2. Toast the flour in your oven by spreading it over your lined baking sheet, and bake in the oven for ten minutes. All to cool completely.   Sift together the flour, baking soda, sugar, cinnamon, and salt.
3. In another bowl, beat the oil with the maple syrup and vanilla.
4. Add the two mixtures together to form a dough.
5. Mix two tablespoons of water into the dough, then let rest for five minutes.
6. Tip onto a floured surface, and shape into a rectangle. Roll until about a quarter-inch thick, and measuring roughly 14 x 10 inches.
7. Prick all over with a fork and score squares, then transfer toa lined baking sheet.
8. Bake for around twelve minutes. Cool completely before snapping them apart along the scored lines.

Lemon Scones

Time: 25mins   **Serves:** 8-12

INGREDIENTS

- 2tbsp. baking powder
- 1/2tsp. salt
- 1/2 cup sugar
- 1/3 cup sunflower oil
- 3 cups all-purpose flour
- 2tsp. lemon extract
- 11/2 cups unsweetened soymilk

METHOD

1. Preheat your oven to 400°F.
2. Combine the dry ingredients in one bowl, and the wet ingredients in another.
3. Gently combine the two mixtures.
4. Rough out the dough on a floured surface, then cut into 8-12 scones.
5. Bake for fifteen minutes, or until the tops are firm.

Banana and Flaxseed Muffins

Time: 25mins   **Serves:** 12

INGREDIENTS

- 2 cups whole wheat flour
- 1/4tsp. salt
- 1/2 cup sugar
- 1tbsp. egg substitute
- 2tsp. baking powder
- 1/4 cup flaxseed meal
- 1tsp. vanilla extract
- 11/4 cups soymilk
- 1/4 cup refined coconut oil, melted
- 1/2tsp. butter pecan flavoring
- 1/2 cup chopped nuts
- 2 large bananas

METHOD

1. Preheat your oven to 375°F, and grease a muffin pan.
2. Sift together the sugar, flour, baking powder, egg replacer, salt, and flaxseed meal.
3. In another bowl, beat the soymilk with the vanilla, oil, and butter pecan flavoring.
Stir in the dry mix, then fold in the bananas.
4. Divide between your muffin cups, and bake for fifteen minutes.

Bread Machine Bread

Time: 3hrs 10mins**Serves:** 1

INGREDIENTS

- 1tbsp. olive oil
- egg substitute (equivalent to 1 egg)
- 3tbsp. maple syrup
- 1/2tsp. vanilla
- 11/4 cups bread flour
- 1 cup whole wheat flour
- 1/2 cup warm water
- 1 small banana, sliced
- 11/2tsp. dry yeast
- 1/2tsp. salt

METHOD

Chuck everything into your bread machine, and select 'basic bread.'

Bran Flax Muffins

Time: 45mins   **Serves:** 15-18

INGREDIENTS

- ¾ cup ground flaxseeds
- ½ cup wheat germ
- ¾ cup natural bran
- ½ cup brown sugar
- 1tsp. baking powder
- 2tsp. baking soda

- 1tsp. salt
- ¾ cup unsweetened almond milk
- 2tsp. ground cinnamon
- 1 cup whole wheat pastry flour
- 1tsp. vanilla extract

- 2 medium bananas, mashed
- 2 cups shredded zucchini or carrots
- ¾-1½cup raspberries
- ¾ cup applesauce, unsweetened

METHOD

1. Preheat your oven to 350°F, grease a muffin pan.
2. Combine your flaxseed, flour, wheat germ, brown sugar, oat bran, baking soda, salt, baking powder, and cinnamon.
3. In another bowl, mix the milk with the applesauce, vanilla, fruit, and vegetables.
4. Gently combine the two mixtures.
5. Divide among your muffin cups, and bake for eighteen to twenty minutes.

Spiced Almond Bread

Time: 50mins   **Serves:** 12

INGREDIENTS

- ⅓ cup canola oil
- ⅔ cup sugar
- 1 cup soy yogurt

- 1½ cups all-purpose flour
- 1tsp. cinnamon or pumpkin pie spice

- ¼ cup almonds, chopped
- 2tsp. baking powder

METHOD

1. Preheat your oven to 350°F, and grease an 8-inch loaf pan.
2. Combine all your wet ingredients with the sugar.
3. Mix the dry ingredients bar the almonds.
4. Combine the two mixtures, then fold in the almonds.
5. Bake for 40-45 minutes, then allow to cool in the pan.

Awesome Apple Bread

Time: 1hr 20mins   **Serves:** 24

INGREDIENTS

- 1 cup oil
- 2 cups apples, shredded
- ½ cup applesauce
- 2 cups brown sugar

- 1½ cups unbleached flour
- 1tsp. vanilla
- 1 cup whole wheat flour
- 1tsp. cinnamon

- ½ cup ground flaxseeds
- 1tsp. baking soda
- 1 cup walnuts, chopped
- 1tsp. salt

METHOD

1. Preheat your oven to 300°F, and grease two regular loaf pans.
2. Combine all the ingredients, then fold in the walnuts.
3. Blend in walnuts.
4. Divide between the loaf pans, then bake for an hour and a half.

Brilliant Banana and Blueberry Muffins

Time: 40mins   **Serves:** 10-12

INGREDIENTS

- 2 bananas, mashed
- ½tsp. baking powder
- ½ cup white sugar
- ½tsp. salt
- ½ cup whole wheat pastry flour
- ¾ cup all-purpose flour
- 1½tsp. egg substitute (dry)
- ½ cup blueberries
- 2tsbp. water

METHOD

1. Preheat your oven to 350°F, and grease a muffin pan.
2. Mix together your mashed bananas, baking powder, sugar, salt, and flours until smooth.
3. In another bowl, combine the egg replacer and water, then stir this into the banana mix and fold in the blueberries.
4. Divide between your muffin cups, and bake for 20 to 25 minutes.

Gluten-Free Blueberry and Banana Bread

Time: 35mins

INGREDIENTS

- ¼ cup rice milk
- 2tbsp. oil
- 1tsp. stevia powder
- 1 cup rice flour
- ½tsp. salt
- 2tsp. baking powder
- 1tsp. cinnamon
- 1½tsp. Ener-G Egg Substitute (mixed in 2tbsp. water)
- ½tsp. xanthan gum
- ½tsp. nutmeg
- 2 medium bananas, ripe and mashed
- 2tbsp. unsweetened applesauce
- ⅓ cup blueberries

METHOD

1. Preheat your oven to 400°F, and grease a 9x9 pan.
2. Combine the egg with the water, and oil, then set aside.
3. Combine your flour, baking powder, stevia powder, salt, nutmeg, cinnamon, and xanthan gum, then mix in the wet ingredients.
4. Stir in the mashed bananas, blueberries, and applesauce.
5. Bake for 25-30 minutes.

Zucchini Bread

Time: 1hr 20mins   **Serves:** 8

INGREDIENTS

- 3 egg substitute
- 1 cup sugar
- ¾ cup applesauce
- 2tsp. vanilla extract
- 1tbsp. baking soda
- 3 cups flour
- 2 cups zucchini, grated
- 1tbsp. cinnamon
- 1tsp. baking powder
- 2tsp. nutmeg

METHOD

1. Preheat your oven to 350°F, and grease a loaf pan.
2. Combine all your ingredients, then stir in the wets.
3. Bake for 60 to 70 minutes.

Perfect Peanut Bread

Time: 1hr 5mins

INGREDIENTS

- ½ cup cornmeal
- 1½ cups flour
- 3tsp. baking powder
- ¼ cup sugar
- 1 pinch salt
- ½ cup applesauce
- ¼ cup peanut butter
- ½ cup water

METHOD

1. Preheat your oven to 350°F, and grease a loaf pan.
2. Combine your dry ingredients, then mix in the wet ingredients.
3. Bake for an hour.

Delicious Banana and Pecan Bread

Time: 16mins   **Serves:** 12

INGREDIENTS

- ½ cup canola oil
- 1tsp. vanilla extract
- 1 cup packed brown sugar
- 3 bananas, well mashed
- 2tsp. baking powder
- 2 cups flour
- ½tsp. cinnamon
- ¾ cup pecans, slightly toasted and chopped
- ½tsp. salt

METHOD

1. Preheat your oven to 350°F, and grease a loaf pan.
2. Combine all your dry ingredients, then mix in the wet ingredients.
3. Fold in the pecans, and bake for an hour.

'Cheesy' Biscuits

Time: 35mins   **Serves:** 12

INGREDIENTS

STARTER
- 1tbsp. lemon juice

BISCUIT DOUGH
- ½ cup nutritional yeast flakes
- 1tsp. chili powder
- 1tbsp. baking powder
- 2 cups whole wheat pastry flour
- 1 cup plain, unsweetened soymilk
- ¾tsp. salt
- ¼ cup canola oil
- ½tsp. garlic powder

METHOD

1. Preheat your oven to 400°F.
2. Stir the lemon juice into the milk, and let it rest for ten minutes.
3. Combine all the dry ingredients, then fold in the oil until crumbly.
4. Use a fork to stir in enough of soured non-dairy milk to form a dough.
5. Turn onto a -floured surface and knead gently until it is smooth.
6. Roll out until a half-inch thick, and cut into biscuits, then arrange on a baking sheet.
7. Bake for fifteen to eighteen minutes.

Great Corn Muffins

Time: 35mins   **Serves:** 3-4

INGREDIENTS

- ¼lb regular reduced-fat firm tofu
- ¼ cup water
- ¼ cup pure maple syrup
- 1tbsp. canola oil
- ½ cup yellow cornmeal
- ½ cup whole wheat pastry flour
- 1tsp. baking powder
- ¼tsp. salt
- ½tsp. baking soda

METHOD

1. Preheat your oven to 350°F, and grease your muffin pan.
2. In your food processor, blend the maple syrup, tofu, water, and oil until smooth.
3. Combine the remaining ingredients, then stir in the blended mixture.
4. Divide between your muffin cups, and bake for 20 to 25 minutes.

Apple and Cinnamon French Toast

Time: 35mins   **Serves:** 4

INGREDIENTS

- ½ cup unsweetened applesauce
- 2tbsp. light brown sugar or sugar substitute
- ¼ cup drained, soft silken
- tofu
- 1tsp. ground cinnamon
- 2tbsp. canola oil
- 8 slices bread
- 1 cup soymilk
- 1tsp. fresh lemon juice
- 1 large apple, peeled, cored, and thinly sliced

METHOD

1. In your food processor, blend the soymilk, tofu, applesauce, a tablespoon of the brown sugar, and the cinnamon. Submerge the bread in the batter, then cook over a mediumohigh heat until browned.
2. Keep the toast warm in a low oven, and heat a tablespoon of corn oil in the skillet.
3. Add the apple, lemon juice, and the rest of the sugar, and cook until the apples are tender.
4. Serve the toast topped with the apple.

Charming Challah

Time: 2hrs 30mins   **Serves:** 20

INGREDIENTS

- 2½tbsp. dry active yeast
- 3 cups unbleached flour
- 1 cup soy flour
- 3 cups whole wheat pastry flour
- 1tbsp. salt
- ½ cup vegetable oil
- ½ cup brown sugar or artificial sweetener
- 2 overripe bananas,
- mashed
- ⅓ cup lukewarm water
- ½ cup cold water
- 1 cup boiling water

METHOD

1. Dissolve the yeast in the warm water, and leave until active.
2. Combine the sugar, oil, salt, and boiling water. Stir in the cold water, then add the yeast.
3. Add the bananas, then add the flour, one cup at a time.
4. Tip onto a floured surface, and knead for five to ten minutes, until smooth.
5. Leave to prove for an hour, in a greased bowl topped with a tea towel.
6. Preheat your oven to 350°F. Knock the dough back, turn it out of the bowl, and knead again.
7. Divide into two balls, then divide each ball into three. Roll into long ropes, then make two braids.
8. Allow the braids to sit for 45 minutes, then brush with boiled water, and sprinkle with sesame or poppy seeds, then bake until cooked through.

Stove-Top Cornbread

Time: 45mins   **Serves:** 6-8

INGREDIENTS

- ½ cup whole wheat pastry flour
- 1½ cups yellow cornmeal
- 1tbsp. baking powder
- 1 cup unsweetened soymilk
- 1tsp. salt
- 1tbsp. apple cider vinegar
- 2tbsp. warm water
- 1½tsp. Ener-G Egg Substitute
- ⅓ cup Earth Balance non-hydrogenated vegan margarine
- creamed corn
- 2tbsp. honey or other liquid sweetener

METHOD

1. Mix together the flour, cornmeal, baking powder, and salt.
2. Combine the apple cider vinegar and soymilk, and leave to sour.
3. Mix the egg replacer with warm water until smooth, and in another cup, melt a third-cup of margarine.
4. In another bowl, combine the soured soymilk, water/egg replacer mixture, melted margarine, and honey.   Add this to the mixed flour, then add the creamed corn and combined.
5. In a cast-iron skillet over a medium heat, melt a generous amount of margarine, then reduce the temperature to low.   Pour in the batter, cover, and cook for thirty to forty minutes.
6. Once firm throughout, turn off the heat but leave covered for several minutes.

Chocolate Bran Muffins

Time: 35mins

INGREDIENTS

- 1 cup water, warm
- 3tbsp. water
- 1tbsp. ground flaxseed
- ½ cup oil
- 1 cup flour
- 1 cup all-bran cereal
- ¾ cup brown sugar
- 1tsp. baking powder
- ½ cup chocolate chips
- 1tsp. baking soda

METHOD

1. Preheat your oven to 350°F, and grease a muffin pan.
2. Mix the bran and warm water, then allow to rest for three minutes.
3. Simmer the flaxseed in the three tablespoons water until thickened.
4. Blend these two mixes, and the rest of the ingredients, until well combined.
5. Bake for eighteen to twenty minutes.

Carrot, Raisin, and Ginger Muffins

Time: 25mins   **Serves:** 7

INGREDIENTS

- ½ cup sugar
- 1tsp. baking powder
- 1tsp. baking soda
- ½tsp. salt
- 1 cup raisins
- ½tsp. cinnamon
- 2 medium carrots, grated
- 2 cups flour
- 2 eggs, equivalent
- ¾ cup soymilk
- 2tbsp. applesauce
- 2tbsp. ginger, grated
- 2tbsp. oil

METHOD

1. Preheat your oven to 400°F, and grease a muffin pan.
2. Mix all your dry ingredients, then stir in the wet ingredients until combined.
3. Bake for twelve to fifteen minutes.

Apple Crumble Muffins

Time: 42mins   **Serves:** 24

INGREDIENTS

APPLE MIXTURE
- 2 apples, core, peeled and diced
- 1tbsp. maple syrup
- 1tbsp. canola oil
- 1/4tsp. grated nutmeg
- 1/2tsp. ground cinnamon

CRUMB TOPPING
- 1/2 cup sucanat
- 11/4 cups unbleached all-purpose flour
- 1 cup uncooked rolled oats
- 1 pinch salt
- 1/4 cup coconut butter
- 1tsp. ground cinnamon
- 1/2tsp. vanilla extract
- 1/4tsp. grated nutmeg

MUFFINS
- 2tsp. baking powder
- 2 cups unbleached all-purpose flour
- 2tsp. baking soda
- 11/2 cups whole wheat flour
- 1tsp. ground ginger
- 2tsp. ground cinnamon
- 11/4 cups canola oil
- 2 tablespoons vanilla extract
- 11/2 cups maple syrup
- 1tsp. salt
- 11/2 cups water
- 2tbsp. apple cider vinegar

METHOD

1. Preheat your oven to 375°F, and grease a 24-cup muffin pan.
2. Cook the apple mixture ingredients over a medium heat for around five minutes, or until slightly softened.
3. For the crumb topping, gently combine the ingredients, and set aside.
4. Mix together all the dry ingredients for the muffins, then stir in the wet ingredients.
5. Fold in the apple mixture.
6. Divide between your muffin cups, then sprinkle with the crumb topping.
7. Bake for around twenty minutes.

Maple-Glazed Pumpkin Scones

Time: 30mins   **Serves:** 36

INGREDIENTS

Scones
- 7 cups flour
- 11/2 cups brown sugar
- 4tsp. baking powder
- 3tsp. pumpkin pie spice
- 1tsp. baking soda
- 1 cup margarine
- 1/2 cup raisins
- 71/2 cups pumpkin puree

Glaze
- 11/2tbsp. margarine, melted
- 1tbsp. maple syrup
- 1 cup brown sugar
- 1tbsp. soymilk

METHOD

1. Preheat your oven to 425°F, and grease a cookie sheet.
2. Combine all the dry ingredients, then cut in the margarine.
3. Stir in the pumpkin, then tip out onto a floured surface and knead.
4. Shape the dough into triangles.   Bake for ten to twelve minutes.
5. Powder the sugar in your food processor, then stir it into the melted margarine.
6. Add the maple syrup and soymilk, and mix well.
7. Drizzle the glaze over the scones, then cool before serving.

Apple and Raisin Spiced Muffins

Time: 25mins   **Serves:** 10-20

INGREDIENTS

- 1tsp. baking powder
- 1tsp. cinnamon
- ½tsp. baking soda
- ¼tsp. nutmeg
- 1 cup water
- ½tsp. allspice
- 3 cups flour
- ⅓ cup maple syrup
- ½ cup raisins
- 2 apples, cored and chopped

METHOD

1. Preheat your oven to 350°F, and grease your muffin pan.
2. Combine all the ingredients, and bake for twenty minutes.

Cinnamon Buns

Time: 1hr 45mins   **Serves:** 24

INGREDIENTS

- ¼tsp. nutmeg
- 3tsp. active dry yeast
- ½tsp. salt

FILLING

- 2tsp. vanilla extract
- ½ cup vegan margarine
- 2tbsp. sugar
- 4 cups all-purpose flour
- 1tsbp. oil
- 1 cup sugar
- ¼ cup brown rice syrup
- 1 cup tepid water
- 3tbsp. ground cinnamon

METHOD

1. Mix the water, sugar, and yeast, and leave to activate.
2. Combine this with the flour, salt, and nutmeg, and leave to knead in your bread machine until smooth.
3. Leave to prove in an oiled bowl covered in a tea towel, for an hour.
4. Combine the remaining ingredients, and reserve.
5. Knock back your dough, and divide into two balls.
6. Roll each into 9x13-inch rectangles, then divide the filling between the two, and roll up.
7. Slice, then place in a cake pan, and leave to rise for a half-hour.
8. Bake at 350°F for fifteen to twenty minutes.

Banana Biscuits

Time: 30mins   **Serves:** 35

INGREDIENTS

- 1 cup soymilk
- 3 small ripe bananas, peeled and mashed
- 2tbsp. canola oil
- 1tbsp. baking powder
- 4¼ cups unbleached white flour

METHOD

1. Preheat your oven to 425°F, and grease a baking sheet.
2. Combine your mashed bananas, soymilk, and oil.
3. Add the flour and baking powder, and stir well.
4. Turn out onto a floured surface, and knead for three minutes.
5. Roll out until it's a ½-inch thick, then cut into 2-inch-wide circles.
6. Bake for twenty minutes, or until browned.

Fantastic Flat Bread

Time: 25mins **Serves:** 4

INGREDIENTS

BREAD
- 2tsp. baking powder
- ½tsp. salt
- 1tbsp. sugar
- 1 cup soymilk
- 2 cups flour
- 2tbsp. oil

TOPPING
- Salt, to taste
- 2 garlic cloves, minced
- 2tbsp. olive oil
- 1tsp. mixed green herbs

METHOD

1. Preheat your oven to 375°F, and grease a cookie sheet.
2. Combine your dry ingredients, then add the oil and soymilk.
3. Tip onto a floured surface, and knead gently for a minute or two, then flatten on the cookie sheet.
4. Combine the topping ingredients, then smear this over the dough.
5. Bake for twenty minutes, or until golden on top.

Low Fat Chocolate Muffins

Time: 30mins **Serves:** 12

INGREDIENTS

- 1 cup all-purpose flour
- ½ cup granulated sugar
- ½ cup whole wheat flour
- ¼ cup granular Splenda
- 2tsp. baking powder
- ¼ cup unsweetened cocoa powder
- 1tsp. baking soda
- ⅔ cup low-fat vanilla yogurt
- ½tsp. salt
- ⅔ cup soymilk
- ⅓ cup carob chips
- ½tsp. vanilla extract

METHOD

1. Preheat your oven to 400°F, and grease a muffin pan.
2. Combine the sugar, flour, cocoa, baking soda, baking powder, and salt, then add the milk, yogurt, and vanilla extract. Stir until combined, then fold in the chocolate chips.
3. Divide between the muffin cups, then bake for fifteen to twenty minutes.

Ginger and Carrot Muffins

Time: 40mins **Serves:** 8-10

INGREDIENTS

- 1tbsp. baking powder
- 3 cups flour
- 1tsp. salt
- ½ cup soymilk
- 1 cup orange juice
- 1 cup carrot, grated
- ginger
- cinnamon, to taste
- brown sugar
- canola oil cooking spray
- cardamom, to taste

METHOD

1. Preheat your oven to 350°F, and grease a muffin pan.
2. Mix together all your dry ingredients, then stir in the carrot, soymilk, and half the orange juice.
3. Stir in the sugar and spices to your taste.
4. Divide between your muffin cups, then bake for fifteen minutes.

The Simplest Blueberry Muffins Ever

Time: 25mins   **Serves:** 10

INGREDIENTS

- ½ cup sugar
- 1½ cups flour
- 2tsp. baking powder
- 1tsp. salt
- ¾ cup soymilk
- 1 cup frozen blueberries
- ¼ cup oil

METHOD

1. Preheat your oven to 350°F, and grease a muffin pan.
2. Combine all the ingredients, divide between your muffin cups, and bake for twenty minutes.

Nutty Cranberry Muffins

Time: 45mins

INGREDIENTS

- 4 cups all-purpose flour
- ⅔tsp. baking soda
- 4tsp. baking powder
- ⅔tsp. salt
- 1tsp. ginger
- 4tsp. cinnamon
- 2 generous cups cranberries
- 1 cup walnuts, chopped
- 1 apple, diced
- ⅔ cup brown sugar, packed
- 1 ⅔ cups non-dairy milk
- ⅔ cup granulated sugar
- 8tbsp. of the juice from canned chick-peas
- ⅓ cup applesauce
- 1 cup vegetable oil

METHOD

1. Preheat your oven to 375° F, and grease your muffin pan.
2. Combine your baking powder, flour, baking soda, cinnamon, salt, and ginger.
3. In another bowl, combine your nuts, cranberries, diced apple, and both sugars.
4. Froth the chickpea juice with a fork, and mix it with the milk, oil, and applesauce, then combine all this to your dry ingredients. .
5. Fold in the fruit and nut mix, then divide between your muffin cups.
6. Bake for 20 to 25 minutes.

Whole Wheat Cornbread

Time: 30mins   **Serves:** 12

INGREDIENTS

- 2tbsp. ground flaxseeds
- 1 cup whole wheat flour
- 6tbsp. water
- 1 cup cornmeal
- ¼ cup sugar
- ¾tsp. salt
- 4tsp. baking powder
- 1 cup almond milk
- ⅛ cup oil
- ⅛ cup applesauce

METHOD

1. Preheat your oven to 425°F, and grease a square baking pan.
2. Combine your flaxseed and water, and leave to thicken.
3. Combine your cornmeal, flour, sugar, baking powder, and salt.
4. Stir in the flaxseed mix, followed by the applesauce, milk, and oil. Combine.
5. Bake for 20 to 25 minutes, and leave to cool for ten minutes before serving.

Blueberry and Banana Muffins

Time: 28mins   **Serves:** 12

INGREDIENTS

- 3⁄4 cup white whole wheat flour
- 1⁄2 cup white sugar
- 1⁄4 cup light brown sugar
- 1⁄2tsp. salt
- 1⁄3 cup vegetable oil
- 2tsp. baking powder
- 3⁄4 cup all-purpose flour
- 1 large banana, mashed
- 1 cup fresh blueberries
- 1⁄2 cup non-dairy milk

METHOD

1. Preheat your oven to 400°F, and grease your muffin pan.
2. Combine your dry ingredients, then add your wet ingredients, and then fold in the blueberries.
3. Divide between your muffin cups, and bake for around twenty minutes.

Blueberry and Lemon Scones

Time: 25mins   **Serves:** 9-12

INGREDIENTS

- 2tsp. baking powder
- 2 cups whole wheat pastry flour
- 1tsp. lemon zest
- 1⁄4tsp. salt
  GLAZE
- 1⁄2 cup powdered sugar
- 1⁄2tsp. baking soda
- 1⁄3 cup agave nectar
- 1tbsp. lemon juice
- 1 cup soymilk
- 1tbsp. vegan egg replacer
- 1⁄2tsp. lemon zest
- powder, mixed to the equivalent of 1 egg
- 11 cup blueberries
- ⁄4 cup vegan margarine, melted
- 1tbsp. lemon juice

METHOD

1. Preheat your oven to 400°F, and line a baking sheet.
2. Combine all the dry ingredients, then stir in the wet ingredients.
3. Fold in your blueberries, then dollop onto a baking sheet.
4. Bake for fifteen minutes.
5. Meanwhile, combine the glaze ingredients, then drizzle this over the scones while still hot.

Apple and Banana Muffins

Time: 55mins   **Serves:** 12-15

INGREDIENTS

- 4tsp. baking powder
- 1⁄2 cup sugar
- 1⁄2tsp. cinnamon
- 11⁄2 cups apple juice
- 2 cups flour
- 2 ripe bananas, mashed
- 1 apple, diced

METHOD

1. Preheat your the oven to 325°F, and grease a muffin pan.
2. Combine all your dry ingredients, then mix in the apple, banana, and apple juice.
3. Divide between your muffin cups, and bake for 35-45 minutes.

Sweet Potato Muffins

Time: 55mins   **Serves:** 18

INGREDIENTS

- 3 cups gluten-free flour, mix
- 1½tsp. baking soda
- ¾tsp. xanthan gum
- ½tsp. salt
- ½tsp. nutmeg
- 1tsp. cinnamon
- ¼tsp. ginger
- 2 cups sweet potatoes, mashed
- ¼tsp. allspice
- ½ cup vegetable oil
- 1tsp. vanilla
- ¾ cup agave syrup
- ½ cup raisins
- ½ cup walnuts
- ½ cup cranberries

METHOD

1. Preheat your oven to 350°F, and grease a muffin pan.
2. Combine all your dry ingredients, then gentle stir in the wet ingredients.
3. Fold in the raisins and cranberries, then divide between your muffin cups.
4. Bake for 20 to 25 minutes.

Chocolate and Peanut Butter Muffin

Time: 30mins   **Serves:** 10

INGREDIENTS

- 1 cup all-purpose flour
- ⅓ cup cocoa powder
- ⅔ cup quick-cooking oats
- ¾ cup sugar
- 1tsp. salt
- 1tbsp. baking powder
- ½ cup peanut butter
- ¼ cup water
- ¾ cup soymilk

METHOD

1. Preheat your oven to 400°F, and grease a muffin pan.
2. Sift together all your dry ingredients.
3. Heat the soymilk and peanut butter together until the butter is melted, then pour this into your dry ingredients and gently combine.
4. Divide between your muffin cups, and bake for fifteen minutes.

Walnut Wheat Bread

Time: 2hrs 35mins   **Serves:** 36

INGREDIENTS

- 1tbsp. yeast
- 1 cup cracked wheat
- 3 cups warm water, divided
- 3 cups whole wheat flour
- 1tbsp. salt
- 3 cups bread flour
- ⅓ cup molasses
- 3 cups walnuts, toasted and coarsely chopped
- 1 cup raisins

METHOD

1. Line a baking sheet with parchment paper.
2. Activate the yeast in a half-cup of lukewarm water.
3. Add the remaining water, cracked wheat, and wheat flour in large bowl, and stir vigorously.
4. Cover with plastic wrap, and leave to prove for an hour. .
5. Mix in the remaining ingredients, and knead well.
6. Leave to prove until doubled in size.   Preheat your oven to 350°F.
7. Divide your dough into three parts, and form into long flat pieces. Twist each piece into a corkscrew shape, and pop onto your sheet, leaving about two inches between loaves.
8. Allow to rise for another thirty minutes, then bake for 35 minutes.

Toddler's Muffins

Time: 45mins **Serves:** 12

INGREDIENTS

- 1 cup whole wheat flour
- 1½tsp. baking soda
- 2 cups rolled oats
- ¼tsp. salt
- 1¼ cups applesauce
- 1tsp. cinnamon
- 1tbsp. chia seeds
- ⅓ cup coconut oil
- 1tsp. vanilla
- ½ cup brown sugar

METHOD

1. Soak your chia seeds in a quarter-cup of water for ten minutes.
2. Preheat your oven to 350°F, and grease a muffin pan.
3. Combine all your dry ingredients but the oats and sugar.
4. Stir in the oats, then reserve.
5. Combine the coconut oil, applesauce, sugar, and vanilla, then add the chia gel.
6. Combine this with the dry ingredients, and gently stir together.
7. Divide between your muffin cups, and bake for 25 minutes.

Nut and Banana Muffins

Time: 35mins

INGREDIENTS

- ¼ cup peanut butter
- ⅛ cup cinnamon baking chips
- 2 bananas, mashed
- ½ cup coffee
- ⅛ cup semi-sweet
- chocolate chips
- ⅛ cup oats
- 1 ⅓ cups whole wheat flour
- ⅛ cup flax seed, ground
- ⅓ cup flour
- ¼tsp. baking soda
- 1½tsp. baking powder
- ½tsp. cinnamon
- 1 pinch salt
- ⅛tsp. nutmeg

METHOD

1. Preheat your oven to 350°F, and grease a muffin pan.
2. Mix together the bananas, peanut butter, and coffee.
3. Add the cinnamon, chocolate chips, oats, and flaxseeds.
4. In another bowl, mix together the baking powder, flours, baking soda, nutmeg, cinnamon, and salt.
5. Combine these two mixtures together, then divide between your muffin cups.
6. Bake for fifteen to twenty minutes.

Muffin Carrot Cakes

Time: 30mins **Serves:** 12

INGREDIENTS

- ½ cup brown sugar
- 2tsp. cinnamon
- ¼ cup raisins
- 1tsp. baking powder
- ½tsp. nutmeg
- 1tsp. baking soda
- 1½ cups whole wheat flour
- ¼tsp. salt
- 1 cup carrot, shredded
- 1½ cups unsweetened applesauce

METHOD

1. Preheat your oven to 350°F, and grease a muffin pan.
2. Combine the dry ingredients, combine the wet ingredients, then mix these two together.
3. Divide between your muffin cups, and bake for 25 minutes.

Very Berry Muffins

Time: 30mins **Serves:** 12

INGREDIENTS

- 1tbsp. ground flaxseeds
- 1 cup whole wheat flour
- 3tbsp. water
- ½ cup spelt flour
- 2tsp. baking powder
- ½ cup oat flour
- 2tsp. baking soda
- ¾ cup almond milk
- ½ - ¾ cup artificial sweetener
- ⅓ cup applesauce
- 1 cup frozen berries
- 1 teaspoon vanilla extract

METHOD

1. Preheat your oven to 375°F, and grease a muffin pan.
2. Mix your flaxseed and water, and leave to thicken.
3. Combine your dry ingredients, then add the applesauce, flaxseed mix, and milk.
4. Add the remaining wet ingredients, then fold in the berries.
5. Divide between your muffin cups, and bake for 20-25 minutes.

Strawberry, Almond, and Cream Scones

Time: 40mins **Serves:** 9

INGREDIENTS

- ⅓ cup sugar
- ¼tsp. salt
- 2tsp. baking powder
- 2tsp. fresh orange zest
- 2 cups unbleached all-purpose flour
- 1 cup fresh strawberries, finely diced
- 4tbsp. Earth Balance vegan margarine
- ¼ cup sliced almonds
- ⅔ cup plain unsweetened soymilk
- 1tsp. rose water

METHOD

1. Preheat your oven to 425°F, and line a baking sheet with parchment paper.
2. Combine your sugar, flour, baking powder, and salt.
3. Add the orange zest, then cut in the cold Earth Balance until crumbly.
4. Stir in the strawberries and almonds, then add the rosewater.
5. Add just enough soymilk to make the dough smooth.
6. Tip onto a floured surface and knead gently.
7. Roll out to desired thickness, then cut into circles and bake for 20 to 25 minutes.

Orange and Pomegranate Muffins

Time: 45mins **Serves:** 12

INGREDIENTS

- ½ cup sugar
- 2 cups whole wheat flour
- ⅔ cup soymilk
- ½tsp. baking soda
- 1tsp. baking powder
- 1½tbsp. flaxseeds, ground
- 2tbsp. safflower oil
- 3-4tbsp. water
- 1tsp. orange zest
- ⅔ cup pomegranate seeds
- ¼ cup orange juice

METHOD

1. Preheat your oven to 350°F, and grease a muffin pan.
2. Mix the ground flax with the water and whisk vigorously for two minutes, then leave to thicken.
3. Combine the sugar, flours, baking powder, and baking soda.
4. Add all the wet ingredients but the pomegranate seeds and gently mix.
5. Fold in the pomegranate seeds. Divide between your muffin cups, sprinkle with a few extra pomegranate seeds, and bake for 20 to 25 minutes.

Gluten-Free Hemp Bread

Time: 1hr 10mins   **Serves:** 6-8

INGREDIENTS

- 1tbsp. dry active yeast
- 2 ¼ - 2 ½ cups warm water
- 1tsp. unbleached cane sugar
- 1/3 cup maple syrup
- ⅓ cup grapeseed oil
- 1tbsp. apple cider vinegar
- 1 cup teff flour
- 2 cups brown rice flour
- 1 cup hemp flour
- ¾ cup arrowroot
- ¾ cup tapioca flour
- 2tsp. xanthan gum
- ½tsp. baking soda
- 1½tsp. salt

METHOD

1. Activate the yeast in the warm water and a teaspoon of sugar. Leave to proof for around ten minutes, or until foamy.
2. Stir in the maple syrup, oil, and apple cider vinegar.
3. In another bowl, combine the flours, arrowroot powder, xanthan gum, salt, and baking soda.
4. Pour the wet ingredients into this, and whisk gently to form a thick batter.
5. Spoon into a prepared pan, then place in a warm spot and leave to rise for around an hour.
6. Preheat your oven to 350°F.
7. Bake for around an hour, then allow to cool in the tin for ten minutes before tipping onto a wire rack.

Pumpkin Spice Scones

Time: 25mins   **Serves:** 10

INGREDIENTS

- 3 cups all-purpose flour
- ¼ cup sugar
- 2tbsp. baking powder
- ½tsp. salt
- ⅓ cup sunflower oil
- ½tsp. pumpkin pie spice
- 1½ cups pumpkin puree
- 2tsp. brown flax seeds
- 1tsp. apple cider vinegar

METHOD

1. Preheat your oven to 400°F, and grease a cookie sheet.   Combine the dry ingredients
2. Stir in the remaining ingredients, and mix the dough by hand.
3. Divide into scones, and place on your cookie sheet, well-spaced.   Bake for 12-15 minutes.

Walnut Bread with Banana and Chocolate Chips

Time: 1hr 5mins

INGREDIENTS

- ¼ cup margarine
- 1 cup banana, mashed
- 1 cup sugar
- ¼ cup applesauce
- 5tbsp. soy yogurt
- 1tsp. vanilla
- 1½ cups flour
- ½tsp. salt
- ½ cup whole wheat flour
- 1tsp. baking soda
- ⅓ cup walnuts
- ⅓ cup chocolate chips

METHOD

1. Preheat your oven to 350°F, and grease your loaf pan.
2. Cream the sugar with the margarine.
3. Stir in the bananas, applesauce, vanilla, and soy yogurt.
4. Combine the flours, salt and baking soda.
5. Mix the two together gently, then tip into your greased pan.
6. Bake for around an hour, then cool on a wire rack.

Spiced Banana and Chocolate Bread

Time: 1hr 5mins   **Serves:** 8-12

INGREDIENTS

- 1½ cups raw sugar
- 2½ cups unbleached bread flour
- 1tsp. baking powder
- 1tsp. ground cinnamon
- ½tsp. salt
- ⅛tsp. ground cloves
- ⅛tsp. ground nutmeg
- ⅛tsp. ground ginger
- 3½oz. bar of intense dark chocolate, roughly chopped
- ¾ cup apple juice
- 2 large ripe bananas, mashed
- ½ cup vegetable oil
- 1tsp. vinegar
- 1½tsp. vanilla

METHOD

1. Preheat your oven to 350°F, and oil a glass pie pan.
2. Mix the dry ingredients with the chocolate pieces.
3. In another bowl, mix the wet ingredients, including the banana.
4. Combine the two mixtures, and pour into your pan.
5. Bake for 55 minutes, then cool on a wire rack.

Banana, Walnut, and Chocolate Chip Muffins

Time: 43mins   **Serves:** 6-12

INGREDIENTS

- 3 ripe bananas, mashed
- 1tsp. vanilla extract
- 3tbsp. coconut oil, liquified
- ⅓ cup brown rice syrup
- 1½ cups flour
- 2tbsp. molasses
- 1½tsp. baking soda
- 1 dash cardamom
- ½tsp. salt
- 1 dash nutmeg
- ½ cup chocolate chips
- 1 cup walnut pieces

METHOD

1. Preheat your oven to 350°F, and grease your muffin pan.
2. Combine your oil, bananas, sweeteners, and vanilla.   Mix in the rest of the ingredients.
3. Divide between your muffin cups, and bake for 23 minutes.

Raisin Buns

Time: 55mins

INGREDIENTS

- 500g. flour
- 1tsp. cardamom
- 100g. sugar
- 100g. soy margarine
- 60g. yeast
- ⅓ liter soymilk
- 40g. raisins
- ¼ liter water
- 1tbsp. sugar

METHOD

1. Preheat your oven to 430°F, and grease a cookie sheet.
2. Melt the margarine with your soymilk and yeast.
3. Combine all your dry ingredients, then stir in the melted margarine mixture.
4. Fold in the raisins, then turn onto a floured surface.
5. Knead gently, then leave to rise in a warm place for around twenty minutes.
6. Knead for another two to three minutes.
7. Divide into biscuits and place on your cookie sheet. Cover with a tea towel, and allow to rise for another ten minutes.
8. Mix a teaspoon of sugar with water, and brush this over your buns before baking for ten to fifteen minutes.

Date and Banana Muffins

Time: 53mins   **Serves:** 8-10

INGREDIENTS

- 1 cup rice milk
- 4 small overripe bananas, mashed
- 1tbsp. white vinegar
- 3⁄4 cup olive oil
- 11⁄4 cups raw wheat germ
- 2tsp. vanilla extract
- 13⁄4 cups spelt flour
- 1tsp. powdered stevia extract
- 1tsp. salt
- 4tsp. ground cinnamon
- 2tsp. baking powder
- 1⁄2 cup pitted dates, coarsely chopped
- 1⁄2 cup sunflower seeds

METHOD

1. Preheat your oven to 180ºC, and grease your muffin pan.
2. Stir the vinegar into the rice milk, and leave aside to curdle.
3. Combine the mashed bananas with the vanilla extract, olive oil, and rice milk.
4. Mix together the wheat germ, spelt flour, stevia, salt, cinnamon, and baking powder.
5. Mix the two mixtures, then stir in the sunflower kernels and dates.
6. Divide between your muffin cups, and bake for around 25 minutes.
7. Place muffin trays into the oven and bake for 23-26 minutes or until a toothpick comes out clean.
8. Cool for 5 minutes in the trays, remove, and let them cool for 5 minutes+ on a cooling tray.

Cheese Scones

Time: 40mins   **Serves:** 4

INGREDIENTS

- 1 cup whole wheat flour
- 11⁄2 cups oats
- 2tsp. baking powder
- 1tsp. baking soda
- 1tsp. salt
- 2tbsp. Splenda granular
- 1⁄3 cup nonfat soymilk
- 1⁄3 cup water
- 2tsp. vinegar
- 3tbsp. vegan margarine
- 1⁄2 cup low-fat vegan cheese

METHOD

1. Preheat your oven to 375°F, and line a baking sheet. Combine all your dry ingredients in a food processor, then pulse the vegan butter and cheese into it until crumbly.
2. Mix together the water, milk, and vinegar, then stir this into your dry ingredients.
3. Divide into scones, and bake for twenty to thirty minutes.

Pumpkin Spice Bread

Time: 1hr 20mins   **Serves:** 8

INGREDIENTS

- 2tbsp. grapeseed oil
- 2⁄3 cup brown sugar
- 1⁄2 medium apple, cooked
- 1⁄2tsp. cornstarch
- 3tbsp. almond milk
- 1 cup cooked pumpkin
- 11⁄3 cups all-purpose flour
- 1⁄3 cup whole wheat flour
- 11⁄2tbsp. flour
- 1⁄2tsp. baking powder
- 1tsp. baking soda
- 1⁄2tsp. salt
- 1⁄2tsp. ground nutmeg
- 1⁄2tsp. ground cinnamon
- 1⁄4tsp. ground allspice
- 3-4tbsp. water
- 1⁄4tsp. ground cloves

METHOD

1. Preheat your oven to 350°F, and prep a glass loaf pan. Mix your baking soda, flour, and baking powder.
2. Chuck all the other ingredients into a food processor, and blend until smooth.
3. Blend this with your dry ingredients, and pour into your loaf pan.
4. Bake for around an hour, then leave to cool for ten minutes in the pan.
   Cool for 10 minutes in the pan, then tip onto a wire rack to cool completely.

Hot Cross Buns

Time: 2hrs 41mins   **Serves:** 24

INGREDIENTS

- 2tbsp. yeast
- 1 cup soya milk
- ½ cup sugar
- ⅓ cup margarine, melted
  GLAZE
- 1½tsp. lemon zest, finely chopped
- 1-2tbsp. soya milk

- and cooled
- 2tsp. salt
- 1tsp. cinnamon
- 4 egg substitute

- 1⅓ cups confectioners' sugar
- ½tsp. lemon extract

- ½tsp. nutmeg
- 5 cups whole wheat flour
- 11 egg white substitute
- ⅓ cups currants or raisins

METHOD

1. Warm your soya milk, then sprinkle in the yeast. Leave to activate for five minutes.
2. Fit your mixer with a dough hook and set at a low speed. Add the yeast, then the sugar, margarine, salt, cinnamon, nutmeg, and "eggs."   Add the flour bit by bit, until the dough is smooth.
3. Detach the bowl, cover with plastic wrap, and leave to prove for around 45 minutes.
4. Knead for another few minutes with the mixer, then add the currants.
5. Shape into a ball, place in a greased dish, and cover again with plastic wrap.
6. Leave it to prove overnight in the fridge, and all the excess moisture will be absorbed by morning.
7. Bring it back to room temperature, then divide into 24 balls and pop onto a lined baking pan.
8. Cover, and leave in a warm place to rise until doubled in size, around an hour and a half.
9. Preheat your oven to 200°C.
10. Slash the buns with a knife, then brush with egg white replacement, and bake for ten minutes.
11. Reduce the heat to 180°C, and cook for another fifteen minutes, then transfer to a wire rack.
12. Mix together all the glaze ingredients, and spoon over your buns in a cross pattern.

Chocolate and Zucchini Bread

Time: 1hr 25mins

INGREDIENTS

- 1 cup water
- 1 cup vegan honey
- 2tbsp. water
- 2 cups coconut oil
- 6 cups buckwheat flour

- 4-5 cups zucchini, shredded
- 3tsp. baking soda
- 6tbsp. ground flaxseeds
- 2tsp. salt

- 2tsp. baking powder
- 1tbsp. cinnamon
- 12oz. package miniature semisweet vegan chocolate chips
- 1tbsp. vanilla

METHOD

1. Preheat your oven to 325°F, and grease four loaf pans. .
2. Mix your flaxseed and water, then leave to thicken for five minutes.
3. Add the vegan honey and beat well. Stir in the zucchini, then mix in the remaining ingredients.
4. Bake in your greased pans for an hour.

Vegan Biscuits

Time: 20mins   **Serves:** 5-8

INGREDIENTS

- 2 cups self-rising flour
- ⅔ cup non-dairy milk substitute

- ¼ cup vegan shortening, such as Earth Balance

METHOD

1. Preheat your the oven to 450°F, and grease a cookie sheet.

Cut the shortening into the flour, then stir in the milk. Roll into two inch balls, and cook for ten minutes.

Dutch Bread

Time: 2hrs 10mins   **Serves:** 30

INGREDIENTS

- 2 cups whole wheat flour
- 2 cups Red River hot cereal, uncooked
- 2⅔ cups water
- 1tsp. baking soda
- 1tsp. baking powder
- ⅓tsp. salt
- ⅓ cup maple syrup
- ⅓ cup molasses

METHOD

1. Preheat your oven to 300°F, and line two loaf pans.
2. Mix together all the ingredients, and divide between your pans.
3. Cover with aluminum foil, and bake for an hour and a half.

Roast Almond and Date Muffins

Time: 35mins

INGREDIENTS

- 250g. whole wheat flour
- 2tsp. baking powder
- 8tbsp. sucanat
- ¼tsp. salt
- 300ml. soya milk
- 1tbsp. Ener-G Egg Substitute
- 4tbsp. coconut oil
- 1tsp. vanilla essence
- 60g. almonds, chopped
- 150g. dates, chopped

METHOD

1. Preheat your oven to 190°C, and spread your almonds at the bottom of a baking tray. Grease a muffin pan.
2. Toast the almonds for five to seven minutes.
3. In your food processor, pulse together the Sucanat, flour, baking powder, salt and egg replacer.
4. In a bowl, blend the vanilla, four tablespoons of oil, and the soya milk.
5. Combine the two mixtures, then fold in the fruit.
1. Divide between your muffin cups, and bake for fifteen to twenty minutes.

Cranberry, Walnut, and Pumpkin Muffins

Time: 45mins

INGREDIENTS

- 1½tsp. salt
- 3½ cups flour
- 1 cup vegetable oil
- 6tsp. baking soda
- 1tsp. cinnamon
- ⅔ cup water
- 3 cups sugar
- 2 cups pumpkin
- 1 cup silken tofu
- 1 cup fresh cranberries
- ½ cup chopped walnuts

METHOD

1. Preheat your oven to 350°F, and grease a muffin pan.
2. Mix the dry ingredients together, mix the wet ingredients together, then combine the two.
3. Fold in the walnuts and cranberries.
4. Divide between the muffin cups, and bake for thirty minutes.

Whole-Grain Pumpkin Muffins

Time: 35mins   **Serves:** 12

INGREDIENTS

- ¾ cup whole wheat pastry flour
- 1 cup oat flour
- ¼ cups unrefined sugar
- ¼tsp. salt
- 1tbsp. baking powder
- 2tsp. pumpkin pie spice
- ½ cup soymilk
- 1 cup pumpkin puree
- ½ cup applesauce
- 2tbsp. molasses
- 1tsp. vegetable oil

METHOD

1. Preheat your oven to 400°F, and grease a muffin pan.
2. Combine your sugar, flour, baking powder, and pumpkin pie spice.
3. Combine the soy milk, pumpkin, applesauce, oil, and molasses.
4. Combine the two mixtures, then divide between your muffin cups and bake for around twenty minutes.

Vegan Bread Machine Bread

Time: 3hrs 5mins   **Serves:** 12

INGREDIENTS

- 12oz. warm water
- 35⁄8 cups whole wheat flour
- 2tbsp. molasses
- 5tsp. vital wheat gluten
- 2tsp. yeast
- 1½tsp. salt

METHOD

1. Pop all the wet ingredients, then all the dry ingredients into your machine.
2. Set the machine for a whole wheat, light loaf, ½ pound setting, and leave to cook.

Graham-Cracker Muffins

Time: 30mins   **Serves:** 12

INGREDIENTS

- ¼ cup sugar
- 1 cup soymilk
- 2tsp. baking powder
- 1½tsp. egg substitute (Ener-G)
- 2 cups graham crackers, crushed
- 2tbsp. vegan honey
- 2tbsp. filtered water (add to egg replacer)

METHOD

1. Preheat your oven to 400°F, and grease a muffin pan.
2. Combine your graham cracker crumbs, sugar, and baking powder.
3. In a separate bowl, combine the milk, egg replacement, and vegan honey.
4. Gentle combine the two to form a batter, and divide between your muffin cups.
5. Bake for around minutes.

Chocolate and Walnut Muffins

Time: 33mins   **Serves:** 8

INGREDIENTS

- ¼ cup cocoa powder
- ½tsp. baking powder
- ½tsp. baking soda
- ½tsp. salt
- 1¼ cups whole wheat flour
- ½ cup vanilla-flavored soymilk
- ¾ cup light maple syrup
- 2tbsp. vegetable oil
- 8 walnut halves
- ½ cup chopped walnuts, plus

METHOD

1. Preheat your oven to 350°F, and grease a muffin pan.
2. Combine your cocoa, flour, baking soda, baking powder, and salt.
3. In another bowl, combine the soymilk, maple syrup, and vegetable oil.
4. Mix together the two mixes, then fold in the walnuts.
5. Divide between your muffin cups, and bake for around twenty minutes.

Busy Muffins

Time: 50mins

INGREDIENTS

- 1 cup all-purpose flour
- 1tbsp. stevia
- ¼ cup sugar
- 2tsp. baking powder
- ½tsp. baking soda
- 1tbsp. cinnamon
- 2 cups whole wheat pastry flour
- ½tsp. salt
- ½ cup applesauce
- ½ cup soymilk, mixed with 3-4 drops lemon juice
- 1 ripe banana, mashed
- 1 small apple, chopped
- 2tbsp. cornstarch, beaten with 2tbsp. water
- 1 small carrot, grated
- ¼ cup walnuts, chopped
- ½ cup raisins

METHOD

1. Preheat your oven to 375°F, and grease a muffin pan.
2. Combine the sugar, flour, stevia, cinnamon, baking powder, baking soda, and salt. Stir in the apple, raisins, carrot, and walnut.
3. Combine the soymilk/lemon, banana, applesauce, and cornstarch mixture.
4. Combine the two ingredients, and divide between the muffin cups.
5. Bake for twenty minutes.

Choca-Mocha Muffins

Time: 35mins   **Serves:** 12

INGREDIENTS

- ¼ cup sugar
- 1½ cups whole wheat pastry flour
- 1tbsp. stevia
- 2tbsp. instant coffee
- ¼ cup baking cocoa
- 2½tsp. baking powder
- 1¼ cups soymilk
- 1tbsp. salt
- ½ cup applesauce
- ½ cup semi-sweet chocolate chips
- 1tsp. vanilla extract

METHOD

1. Preheat your oven to 375°F, and grease a muffin pan.
2. Sift together all your dry ingredients.   Beat together your wet ingredients.
3. Combine the two mixtures, and fold in the chocolate chips.
4. Bake for around twenty minutes.

Chocolate Chip Scones

Time: 40mins

INGREDIENTS

- 3tbsp. sugar
- ½ cup soymilk
- ½ cup vegetable shortening
- ¼ cup soft silken tofu
- 2 cups self-rising flour
- ½ cup semi-sweet chocolate chips
- 1tsp. vanilla extract

METHOD

1. Preheat your oven to 425°F, and grease a large baking sheet.
2. Combine the flour and sugar, then cut in the shortening until it forms crumbs.
3. Beat the soymilk, tofu, and vanilla, then mix with the crumb mix to form dough.
4. Turn onto a floured surface, and knead gently.
5. Roll into a seven inch circle, and cut into eight wedges.
6. Prick all over with a fork, then bake for around twenty minutes.

Cookies

Time: 25mins   **Serves:** 6

INGREDIENTS

- ¾ cup cake flour
- 1 cup quick-cooking rolled oats
- 1 cup walnuts, chopped
- ¼tsp. salt
- 1 cup semisweet vegan chocolate chips
- ¼tsp. baking powder
- ½ cup maple syrup
- ½ cup applesauce
- 2tbsp. water
- ¼ cup cream of wheat
- 2tsp. vanilla extract

METHOD

1. Line two baking sheets with parchment paper.
2. Combine the dry ingredients, then the wet ingredients, then mix together.
3. Let sit five minutes.
4. Drop slightly rounded tablespoons of dough onto baking sheets, about 1 inch apart. Bake one sheet at a time on the center rack of oven until cookies are slightly golden, about 10-15 minutes. Caution, cookies bake very quickly.

Fig and Apple Bran Muffins

Time: 33mins   **Serves:** 12

INGREDIENTS

- ¾ cup fig
- 1 large apple
- 3tbsp. vegetable oil
- 1 cup all-purpose flour
- 1½ cups all-bran cereal
- 1¼ cups apple juice
- 3tbsp. unsweetened applesauce
- ⅓ cup sugar
- ¾tsp. ground cinnamon
- 2tsp. baking powder

METHOD

1. Preheat your oven to 400°F, and grease your muffin pan.
2. Mix together the cereal and apple juice, then leave to stand.
3. Peel, core, and grate the apples. Chop the figs.
4. Add these to the cereal and apple juice, then add the applesauce and oil.
5. Slowly sift in the dry ingredients and mix.
6. Divide between the muffin cups, and bake for eighteen minutes.

Rice Flour and Applesauce Muffins

Time: 20mins

INGREDIENTS

- 3tsp. baking powder
- 1/4tsp. cinnamon
- 1/8tsp. stevia powder
- 1/4tsp. nutmeg
- 1 cup rice milk
- 11/2tsp. Ener-G Egg Substitute (mixed in 2tbsp water)
- 2 cups brown rice flour
- 1/4 cup vegan butter, melted
- 1/2 cup unsweetened applesauce
- 1tsp. vanilla

METHOD

1. Preheat your oven to 375°F, and grease a muffin pan.
2. Combine all the ingredients gently, then divide between the muffin cups.
3. Bake for fifteen to twenty minutes.

Mixed Fruit Muffins

Time: 55mins   **Serves:** 6

INGREDIENTS

- 2 cups oat flour
- 3tsp.baking powder
- 1/2tsp. salt
- 1/2 cup artificial sweetener
- 1/4 cup oil
- 6tbsp. applesauce
- 3/4 cup soymilk mixed with 1tsp vinegar
- 1-2tbsp. ground flaxseeds
- 11/2 cups fruit

METHOD

1. Preheat your oven to 350°F, and grease a muffin pan.
2. Combine the salt, baking powder, flour, and flax.
3. Stir in the egg replacer, sweetener, oil, sour soymilk, and fruit.
4. Divide between your muffin cups, and bake for 35-45 minutes.

Fig, Apricot, and Cornmeal Bread

Time: 1hr   **Serves:** 9-12

INGREDIENTS

- 1/4 cup maple syrup
- 3/4 cup soymilk
- 1/4 cup canola oil
- 11/2tsp. vanilla extract
- 1tsp. orange zest
- 1/2tsp. almond extract
- 1 cup cornmeal
- 2 ripe bananas, mashed
- 1tbsp. baking powder
- 1 cup all-purpose flour
- 1tsp. baking soda
- 1tsp. salt
- 1/2tsp. cinnamon
- 12 dried apricots
- 11/2 cups pecans
- 10 dried figs

METHOD

1. Preheat your oven to 350°F, and grease an 8x8-inch baking pan.
2. Add syrup, soymilk, oil, extracts, and zest to the bananas and beat well.
3. Combine the cornmeal, baking powder, flour, baking soda, cinnamon, and salt.
4. Roughly chop the dried fruits and pecans, then stir into the flour mixture.
5. Combine the two ingredients, pour into your prepped pan, and bake for around fifty minutes.

Fruit and Nut Pumpkin Bread

Time: 1hr 10mins

INGREDIENTS

- ¾ cup flour
- ¾ cup whole wheat pastry flour
- 2¼tsp. baking powder
- ½tsp. cinnamon
- ¼tsp. salt
- ½tsp. nutmeg
- ¼tsp. ground cloves
- ½tsp. ground ginger
- ¼ cup walnut oil
- 1 cup pumpkin
- ½ cup maple syrup
- 1tsp. vanilla
- ½ cup walnuts, chopped
- ¼ cup dried currants

METHOD

1. Preheat your oven to 350°F, and grease a loaf pan.
2. Combine all the ingredients, then fold in the raisins and nuts.
3. Bake for 45 minutes.
4. Cool for ten minutes in the pan, then remove to cool completely.

Oat Bran Muffins

Time: 30mins   **Serves:** 12

INGREDIENTS

- ¼ cup brown sugar
- ¼tsp. salt
- 2tsp. baking powder
- 1 cup soymilk (
- ½ cup raisins
- 2 cups oat bran
- 4oz. egg substitute (for 2 eggs)
- ¼ cup molasses
- 2tbsp. unsweetened applesauce

METHOD

1. Preheat your oven to 425°F, and grease your muffin pan.
2. Combine the dry ingredients.
3. Mix together the egg replacer, soymilk, molasses, and applesauce.
4. Mix these together, then fold in the raisins.
5. Divide between the muffin cups, and bake for around fifteen minutes.

Vegan Cakes

Brilliant Banana Cake

Time: 50mins

Serves: 12

INGREDIENTS

- 1½tsp. baking soda
- 2 cups flour
- ½tsp. salt
- ¼ cup oil
- 1 cup sugar
- 4 ripe bananas, mashed
- 1tsp. vanilla
- ¼ cup water

METHOD

1. Preheat your oven to 350°F, and grease a 9-inch square baking pan.
2. Beat all the ingredients together until well combined.
3. Bake for 45 to 50 minutes.

Very Vegan Vanilla Cake

Time: 40mins   **Serves:** 6-9

INGREDIENTS

- 1 cup sugar
- 1½ cups unbleached all-purpose flour
- 1tsp. baking soda
- ½ cup vegetable oil
- ½tsp. salt
- 1 cup soymilk
- 1tbsp. vinegar
- 1tbsp. vanilla extract

METHOD

1. Preheat your oven to 350°F, and line an 8-inch cake pan.
2. Combine the flour, sugar, baking soda, and salt.
3. Stir in the soymilk, vegetable oil, and vanilla extract. Beat well.
4. Add the vinegar, stir, and transfer to the pan.
5. Bake for a half-hour.
6. Cool in the pan for ten minutes, before turning out onto a wire rack to cool completely.

Chocolate Mug Cake

Time: 5mins   **Serves:** 1

INGREDIENTS

- ¼ cup flour
- ½tbsp. unsweetened cocoa powder
- ¼ cup sugar
- ¼tsp. baking soda
- ½tbsp. vegetable oil
- ⅛tsp. salt
- ¾tsp. white vinegar
- ¼ cup water
- ¼tsp. vanilla

METHOD

1. Combine the dry ingredients in a mug or coffee cup.
2. Add the wet ingredients, and wet with a fork.
3. Microwave on half power for 3 minutes.

Delicious Chocolate Cake

Time: 55mins   **Serves:** 8

INGREDIENTS

- 1½ cups white flour
- ½tsp. baking soda
- ⅓ cup unsweetened cocoa powder
- ½tsp. salt
- ½ cup vegetable oil

FROSTING

- ¼ cup peanut butter
- 2oz. unsweetened chocolate
- 3-4tbsp. water

- 1 cup sugar
- 1 cup cold water or 1 cup chilled brewed coffee
- 2tbsp. cider vinegar
- 2tsp. vanilla extract

- 1 cup confectioners' sugar
- 1tsp. vanilla

METHOD

1. Preheat your oven to 375°F, and grease an 8-inch cake pan.
2. Sift together the cocoa, flour, soda, salt and sugar.
3. In another bowl, mix the oil, water, and vanilla.
4. Mix the two together until smooth.
5. Add the vinegar, stir, and transfer to the pan.
6. Bake for around a half-hour.
7. To make the frosting, melt chocolate in a heavy pan on medium heat.
8. Whisk together peanut butter, water, and vanilla.
9. Stir in the sugar, then beat in the melted chocolate. Continue to beat until smooth.
10. Leave the cake to cool completely before frosting.

Carrot Cake

Time: 1hr 23mins   **Serves:** 12

INGREDIENTS

- ½ cup brown sugar
- 1tsp. salt
- 2 cups flour
- 1tsp. cinnamon
- 1tsp. baking soda
- 1tsp. baking powder
- ¾ cup sugar
  CREAM CHEESE FROSTING
- ¼ cup margarine
- 1½ cups powdered sugar

- 3 cups finely-shredded carrots
- ¾ cup applesauce
- ¾ cup vegetable oil
- 2tsp. vanilla
- ½ cup chopped nuts (optional)
- 4 egg substitute (Ener-G)

- 3oz. Better Than Cream Cheese cream cheese substitute
- 1tsp. vanilla

METHOD

1. Preheat your oven to 325°F, and grease and flour a 10x9" cake pan.
2. Stir together the dry ingredients.
3. Add the egg subs, carrots, oil, apple sauce, and vanilla.
4. Beat well, then stir in the nuts.
5. Bake for around fifty minutes.
6. To make the frosting, combine all the ingredients.
7. All the cake to cool completely before frosting.

Crock Pot Chocolate Pudding Cake

Time: 2hrs 35mins   **Serves:** 6

INGREDIENTS

- ½ cup sugar
- 1 cup all-purpose flour
- 2tbsp. cocoa
- ½tsp. salt
- 2tsp. baking powder
- ½ cup soymilk
- 1tsp. vanilla
- 2tbsp. vegetable oil
- ¾ cup packed brown sugar
- 1½ cups hot water
- ¼ cup cocoa

METHOD

1. Grease your Crock Pot.
2. Combine the flour, sugar, cocoa, baking powder, and salt.
3. Stir in the oil, soymilk, and vanilla, and beat until smooth. Pour into your Crock Pot.
4. Mix the brown sugar and remaining quarter-cup cocoa in bowl. Sprinkle over batter.
5. Pour the hot water over everything, a nd do not stir.
6. Cook on high for two hours, then remove the lid and let it stand for a half-hour.

Pumpkin Cake

Time: 1hr 15mins   **Serves:** 16

INGREDIENTS

- ½ cup vegetable oil
- 1tsp. vanilla extract
- ½ cup maple syrup
- 2½ cups flour
- 1tsp. baking soda
- 1tsp. baking powder
- 1tsp. cinnamon
- 1 cup brown sugar
- ½tsp. ginger
- 1tsp. ground cloves
- ½tsp. nutmeg
- 15oz. can pumpkin
- ½tsp. salt

METHOD

1. Preheat your oven to 375°F, and grease   an 8x8 baking pan.
2. Combine your sugar, oil, syrup, and vanilla, until the sugar is dissolved.
3. Separately, sift together the flour, spices, and salt.
4. Combine the two mixtures, along with the pumpkin, then pour into the pan.
5. Bake for around an hour.

Easy Applesauce Cake

Time: 50mins   **Serves:** 16

INGREDIENTS

- ¾ cup sugar
- 2 cups whole wheat flour
- 1½ cups unsweetened applesauce
- ½tsp. salt
- ⅓ cup oil
- 1tsp. cinnamon
- 1½tsp. baking soda

METHOD

1. Preheat your oven to 350°F, and grease an 8-inch dish.
2. Mix together the oil, sugar, and applesauce.
3. Stir in the dry ingredients, and beat until smooth.
4. Bake for 40 to 45 minutes

Spiced Ginger Cake

Time: 45mins   **Serves:** 6-8

INGREDIENTS

- 1 cup white sugar
- ½tsp. salt
- 1tbsp. baking powder
- 1tsp. cinnamon
- ½tsp. allspice
- ½tsp. ginger
- 1½ cups flour (I used unbleached flour)
- ¼tsp. clove
- 1tbsp. white vinegar
- ½ cup raisins
- 1 teaspoon vanilla extract
- 1 cup ginger ale
- ⅓ cup oil

METHOD

1. Preheat your oven to 350°F, and grease an 8x8 pan.
2. Sift together your flour, baking powder, sugar, salt, and spices.
3. Mix in the vanilla, vinegar, oil, and ginger ale, then fold in the raisins.   Bake for around forty minutes.

Zucchini and Cinnamon Cake

Time: 1hr 5mins   **Serves:** 16

INGREDIENTS

- 2½ cups fresh zucchini, grated peeled
- 1 cup canola oil
- 2 ripe bananas, mashed
- 3 cups flour
- 1tsp. salt
- 2 cups sugar
- 1tsp. baking soda
- 1tsp. vanilla extract
- 1tsp. cinnamon

METHOD

1. Preheat your over to 350°F, and grease a Bundt pan. Combine your zucchini, oil, bananas, and vanilla.
2. Add all the dry ingredients, and mix well. Fold in the chocolate chips and walnuts.
3. Transfer to your pan, and bake for 45 minutes to an hour.
4. Cool for fifteen minutes in your pan, then transfer to a wire rack.

Frosted Raspberry Blackout Cake

Time: 1hr 20mins   **Serves:** 12

INGREDIENTS

- ½ cup cocoa powder
- 1½ cups all-purpose flour
- 1tsp. baking powder
- 1tp. baking soda
- ½tsp. salt
- ½ cup canola oil
- 1½ cups soymilk
- 10oz. jar raspberry preserves
- 1¼ cups sugar
- 2tsp. vanilla extract
- ¾ cup vegan coffee
- creamer
- 10oz. semi-sweet chocolate chips
- 6tbsp. vegan margarine
- fresh raspberry, to decorate

METHOD

1. Bring the creamer to a boil over a medium heat, the stir in the margarine, and keep stirring until melted and combined.
2. Take off the heat, stir in the chocolate chips until melted, then leave to rest for an hour or so.
3. Preheat your oven to 350°F, and grease two 8-inch round cake pans.
4. Combine your flour, baking powder, cocoa powder, baking soda, and salt.
5. In another bowl, combine the rice milk, a half- cup of the preserves, oil, vanilla, and the sugar.
6. Mix with the dry ingredients until well combined and smooth.
7. Divide between your pans, and bake for around 45 minutes.
8. Allow to cool completely before filling and decorating with the ganache and fresh raspberries.

Simple Vanilla Cake

Time: 50mins   **Serves:** 12

INGREDIENTS

- 2¼ cups whole spelt flour
- 1 pinch salt
- 3tsp. baking powder
- ½ cup maple syrup
- 1tsp. lemon zest
- ⅓ cup canola oil
- 1 cup rice milk
- 2tsp. vanilla extract

METHOD

1. Preheat your oven to 350°F, and grease a 9-inch cake pan.
2. Combine your dry ingredients, then mix in the wet ingredients until well combined.
3. Cook in your oven for forty minutes.
4. Cool in the pan for ten minutes, then remove and leave to cool completely.

Lemon Genoise Cake

Time: 50mins   **Serves:** 10-12

INGREDIENTS

- 2tbsp. white flour
- ½tsp. baking soda
- ½ cups granulated sugar
- 2tsp. baking powder
- ¾tsp. salt
- 2tbsp. margarine
- ¼ cup margarine
- 2½ cups white flour
- 2tbsp. lemon juice
- 1 large lemon, zest of
- 1 cup water
- ¾ cup soymilk
- 1tsp. lemon extract
- 1½tsp. vanilla

METHOD

1. Preheat your oven to 350°F, and grease two pans.
2. Mix all the ingredients together well, then divide between your pans.
3. Bake until cooked through.
4. Cool completely in the pan for ten minutes, then turn onto a rack.

Iced Chocolate Cake

Time: 50mins   **Serves:** 12

INGREDIENTS

- 2 cups sugar
- 3 cups flour
- 1tsp. salt
- 2tsp. baking soda
- 1 cup cocoa powder
- 1 cup soymilk
- 2 egg substitute
- ¾ cup light oil
- 1 cup boiling water
- 2tsp. vanilla extract

FOR THE CREAM CHEESE ICING

- 8oz. vegan cream cheese
- ¼ cup margarine
- ½tsp. vanilla extract
- ⅛tsp. salt
- ¾ cup cocoa
- 3¾ cups powdered sugar

METHOD

1. Preheat your oven to 350'F, and grease two 8-inch pans.
2. If you use 2 round 8" cake pans bake for 30-35 minutes.
3. Combine all the ingredients and beat well.
4. Bake for around half an hour.   Allow to cool completely before icing.
   FOR THE CREAM CHEESE ICING:
1. Beat together the margarine, cream cheese, vanilla, and salt.
2. Stir in the cocoa and mix thoroughly.

Apple and Walnut Cake

Time: 1hr 40mins   **Serves:** 16

INGREDIENTS

- 1½ cups vegetable oil
- 2 egg substitute
- 2 cups granulated sugar
- 3tbsp. vanilla
- 1½ cups wheat flour
- 1½ cups all-purpose flour
- 1½tsp. baking soda
- 1tsp. cinnamon
- 1tsp. salt
- ¼tsp. allspice
- 3 cups apples, diced
- 1 cup walnuts, chopped

METHOD

1. Preheat your oven to 350°F, and grease a cake pan.
2. Combine the sugar, oil, egg substitute, and vanilla.
3. Mix the baking soda, flour, and salt.
4. Thoroughly combine the two mixtures, then fold in the nuts and fruit.
5. Bake for an hour and fifteen minutes.

Carrot Cake

Time: 1hr 30mins   **Serves:** 24

INGREDIENTS

- 1 cup sugar
- 1tsp. salt
- 2 cups flour
- 1tsp. cinnamon
- 3tsp. baking powder
- 1 cup brown sugar, packed
- 1tsp. baking soda
- 1½ cups vegetable oil
- 3 cups carrots, shredded
- 2tsp. vanilla
- ½ cup chopped nuts
- 1 cup soft tofu

METHOD

1. Preheat your oven to 325°F, and grease a 13" X 9" pan.
2. Combine all the ingredients well, then fold in the carrots and nuts.
3. Bake for around an hour.

Perfect Pineapple Upside-Down Cake

Time: 1hr   **Serves:** 12

INGREDIENTS

- 1½ cups all-purpose flour
- 1tsp. baking soda
- ½ cup vegan sugar
- ½tsp. salt
- 1tbsp. white vinegar
- ⅓ cup canola oil
- 20oz. pineapple slices
- ¼ cup brown sugar
- 7 cherries

METHOD

1. Preheat your oven to 350°F.
2. Arrange your pineapple slices on the bottom of a 12-inch pan, and put a cherry in the middle of each pineapple ring. Sprinkle with the brown sugar.
3. Combine your dry ingredients.
4. Make up your pineapple juice to one cup using water, then add to the dry ingredients, along with the oil and vinegar.
5. Pour over the pineapple, then bake for around forty minutes.
6. Allow to cool for twenty minutes before removing from the pan.

Simple Apple Sponge Cake

Time: 1hr 10mins   **Serves:** 4-6

INGREDIENTS

- ¾ cup powdered sugar
- 1 cup all-purpose flour
- 1 golden delicious apple,
- peeled cored and pureed
- ½ cup soymilk
- ¼ vegetable oil
- 2tbsp. baking powder
- vanilla essence
- ¼tbsp. salt

METHOD

1. Preheat your oven to 350°F, and grease a cake pan.
2. Combine your salt, flour, and baking powder.
3. In your food processor, blend the pureed apple, vegetable oil, essence, and powdered sugar.
4. Add the milk and your flour mixture, and blend until combined.   Bake for around a half hour.

Upside-Down Banana Cake

Time: 1hr 10mins   **Serves:** 8

INGREDIENTS

Topping
- 2tbsp. lemon juice
- ½ cup packed brown sugar

Cake
- 1 cup raw sugar
- egg replacement equivalent to 2 egg
- 1 cup soymilk

- 1tbsp. vegan margarine
- 2 medium firm bananas,

- 1tsp. vanilla
- 3 ripe bananas, mashed
- 2 cups all-purpose flour
- 3tsp. oil

- sliced
- ½ cup pecan halves

- 1tsp. baking soda
- ¼tsp. salt
- 1tsp. baking powder

METHOD

1. Preheat your oven to 350°F.
2. In a saucepan, mix together the lemon juice, brown sugar, and butter.
3. Bring to a boil, then reduce the heat and leave the sugar to dissolve without stirring.
4. Pour half of this into the bottom of your cake pan, then cover with nuts.
5. Coat your bananas in the remaining mixture, then arrange them over the nuts.
6. Mix together the rest of the ingredients, then pour over the bananas.
7. Bake for around fifty minutes.

Choco-Banana Cake

Time: 55mins   **Serves:** 8

INGREDIENTS

- ⅔ cup maple syrup
- 2tbsp. egg substitute
- ½ cup vegetable oil

- 1tbsp. soy lecithin
- 2 cups whole wheat pastry flour
- 3 ripe bananas, mashed

- 1tsp. baking soda
- ½ cup semisweet vegan chocolate chips
- 1 pinch salt

METHOD

1. Preheat your oven to 350°F.
2. Cream your syrup with the oil and egg replacer.   Stir in the lecithin and bananas.
3. Add the remaining ingredients, and gently mix.
4. Pour into an ungreased 8-inch cake or Bundt pan.   Bake for around forty minutes.

Gooey Chocolate Cake

Time: 50mins

INGREDIENTS

- 2 cups sugar
- 1tsp. salt
- 1⁄2 cup cocoa
- 2tsp. baking soda
- 1tsp. vanilla
- 3 cups flour
- 2tbsp. white vinegar
- 2⁄3 cup oil
- 3⁄4 cup applesauce
- 11⁄4 cups water

METHOD

1. Preheat your oven to 350°F, and grease a 9x14 cake pan.
2. Mix all the dry ingredients.
3. Add the rest of the ingredients, and beat well.
4. Bake for 35 to 40 minutes.

Carrot and Applesauce Cake

Time: 1hr 15mins   **Serves:** 10

INGREDIENTS

- 2 cups carrots, grated
- 2 egg substitute
- 2 cups water
- 11⁄4 cups maple syrup
- 11⁄2tsp. cinnamon
- 3tbsp. vegetable oil
- 3tbsp. unsweetened applesauce
- 11⁄2tsp. allspice
- 11⁄2 cups raisins
- 11⁄2tsp. salt
- 1⁄2tsp. ground cloves
- 3 cups spelt flour
- 3⁄4 cup walnuts, chopped
- 11⁄2 teaspoons baking soda

METHOD

1. Preheat your oven to 350°F, and grease a 9-inch pan.
2. In a large sauce pan, simmer the raisins and carrots in the water over medium heat, for 7 to 10 minutes.
3. Remove from the heat, then add the apple sauce, oil, egg replacers, cinnamon, syrup, allspice, cloves, and salt.
4. Sift in the dry ingredients, and combine.
5. Bake for 45 minutes to an hour.

Banana and Chocolate Cake

Time: 1hr 10mins   **Serves:** 10

INGREDIENTS

- 6tbsp. vegetable oil
- 1⁄4-1⁄2 cup brown sugar
- 3oz. chocolate pieces
- 5 small bananas, mashed
- 3tsp. baking powder
- 2 cups flour
- 1⁄8tsp. salt
- 1⁄4tsp. ground nutmeg
- 1⁄2tsp. ground cinnamon
- 1⁄8tsp. ground cloves
- 3⁄4 cup raisins
- 3⁄4 cup mixed nuts, roughly chopped

METHOD

1. Preheat your oven to 375°F, and grease your pan.
2. Melt the chocolate and dissolve the sugar in the oil over a medium heat.
3. Remove pan the heat, then stir in the nuts and raisins, followed by the mashed banana.
4. Mix in all the dry ingredients, then pour into your cake pan.
5. Bake until a skewer inserted into the middle comes out clean.

Pumpkin Spice Cake with Chocolate Ganache

Time: 45mins   **Serves:** 12-16

INGREDIENTS

- ¼ cup chocolate chips, melted
- 1tsp. vanilla
- ⅔ cup pumpkin
- 2tbsp. canola oil
  GANACHE
- ¾ cup chocolate chips

- 1¼ cups flour
- 2tbsp. Ener-G Egg Substitute
- ¼ cup cocoa powder
- ½tsp. baking powder
- ¼ cup soymilk

- 1½tsp. baking soda
- ¼tsp. salt
- ¼tsp. nutmeg
- 1½tsp. cinnamon
- 3tbsp. margarine

METHOD

1. Preheat your oven to 350°F, and grease a 9x9 pan.
2. Stir the vanilla, pumpkin, oil and egg replacer into the melted chocolate.
3. Sift together the dry ingredients, then mix into the chocolate and pumpkin mix.
4. Pour into your bake, and bake for around 25 minutes.
5. To make the ganache, melt the margarine and soymilk in a bowl, then add the chocolate and stir until melted and smooth.   Leave the cake to cool completely before spreading on the ganache.

Fabulous Chocolate Fudge Cake

Time: 50mins   **Serves:** 8-10

INGREDIENTS

Frosting
- 7oz. bittersweet chocolate, melted
- 1tsp. vanilla extract

Cake
- 1½ cups granulated sugar
- ¾ cup cocoa powder
- ½tsp. salt

- 14oz. can full-fat coconut milk
- ½ cup powdered sugar

- 1¾tsp. baking soda
- 2⅓ cups all-purpose flour
- ½ cup vegetable oil

- 1¾ cups hot coffee

METHOD

1. Pop the coconut milk can in the refrigerator overnight, so the cream separates and hardens.
2. Open the can from the bottom, and pour out the liquid, leaving the hardened coconut cream behind.
3. Scoop the cream into a bowl and stir in the melted chocolate, powdered sugar, and vanilla extract. Beat until smooth, the refrigerate until reader.
4. Preheat your oven to 350°F, and grease two 6-inch cake tins.
5. Combine the sugar, cocoa powder, flour, salt, and baking soda. Add the hot coffee and vegetable oil.
6. Divide between your cake pans, then bake for around a half-hour.
7. Cool in the tin for ten minutes, then turn onto a wire rack.
8. Leave to cool completely before covering with ganache.

Duncan Hines Vegan Box Cakes

Time: 43mins   **Serves:** 4-5

INGREDIENTS

- 43g Duncan Hines cake mix

- 10fl. oz. soda of your choice

METHOD

1. Preheat your oven to 350°F, and grease your pan.   Place the Duncan Hines mix in a container .
2. Add the soda slowly, stirring continuously. Don't add the eggs, water, or oil as per the box instructions.
3. Bake for around half an hour, then let it cool for five minutes before turning it out of the tin.

Grain-Free No-Bake Silk Chocolate and Coconut Cake

Time: 20mins   **Serves:** 6

INGREDIENTS

- 1½ cups walnuts
  CHOCOLATE LAYER
- ⅓ cup pure cocoa powder
- 2tsp. pure vanilla extract
- ¼ cup agave nectar
  COCONUT LAYER
- 1tbsp. agave nectar
- 30oz. can full-fat coconut milk, refrigerated overnight

- 8 pitted medjool dates
- 10½oz. gluten-free medium firm tofu.
- ¼tsp. sea salt

- 1tsp. pure vanilla extract
- 1 cup berries, to garnish
- 2 cups frozen assorted berries

- 2tbsp. pure cocoa powder
- ⅔ cup gluten-free semisweet chocolate chips
- 1tbsp. coconut oil

METHOD

1. Line the bottom of 7-inch spring-form cake pan with parchment paper.
2. In a food processor, blitz your nuts, dates, and cocoa into fine crumbs.
3. Press into the base of your pan, and freeze while you prepare the rest of the cake.
4. For the chocolate layer, blend the tofu until smooth, then add the cocoa, vanilla, agave, and salt, and blend until combined.
5. Melt the coconut oil and chocolate chips together, then add to the tofu mix and blend until smooth.
6. Pour over the crust, and return to the freezer.
7. For the coconut cream layer, remove just the firm part of the coconut milk can, discarding the liquid.
8. Whip until fluffy and soft peaks form, then add the vanilla and agave.
9. Spread over the chocolate layer, then decorate with frozen berries.

Chocolate Lava Cake

Time: 30mins

INGREDIENTS

- 62.5ml. maple syrup
- 94g. gluten-free baking mix
- 25g. unsweetened cocoa

- powder
- ½tsp. baking powder
- ¼tsp. salt
- 185ml. coconut milk

- ⅓tsp. baking soda
- 62.5ml. coconut oil
- 22g. dark chocolate chips
- 1tsp. vanilla extract

METHOD

1. Preheat your oven to 325°F, and grease a muffin pan.
2. Beat the gluten-free baking mix, salt, cocoa powder, baking powder, and baking soda.
3. Add the maple syrup, oil, and vanilla, and beat again. Slowly add the milk, and combine.
4. Divide between your muffin cups, then drop chocolate chips into each.   Bake for 20 to 25 minutes.

Lighter Choco-Banana Cake

Time: 40mins   **Serves:** 12

INGREDIENTS

- 2 cups almond milk
- 1 banana, mashed
- 1 cup sugar
- 1tbsp. baking powder

- 2tbsp. apple cider vinegar
- 2½ cups flour
- 1tbsp. vanilla extract
- ½ cup cocoa powder

- ¼ cup vegetable oil
- ½tbsp. salt

METHOD

Preheat your oven to 350°F, and grease your cake pan. Sift together the flour and cocoa powder, then add all the remaining ingredients, and mix well.   Cook for around 25 minutes.

Not-Quite-Crab Cakes

Time: 20mins **Serves:** 6-8

INGREDIENTS

- 14oz. can chickpeas
- 14oz. can hearts of palm, chopped into large pieces
- 1 jalapeno, seeded and minced
- ¼ cup vegan mayonnaise
- 2tbsp. Old Bay Seasoning
- 1tsp. vinegar, plum
- 1tsp. Dijon mustard
- 1 cup panko breadcrumbs, plus 1/2 cup for coating

METHOD

1. In your food processor, blitz together the hearts of palm, chickpeas, and jalepeño until roughly mashed.
2. Transfer to a bowl, and add the other ingredients. Combine.
3. Place the remaining ½ cup of panko in a shallow dish.
4. Heat an oil coated skillet on medium-high heat.
5. Shape the 'crab' into cakes, then coat in the panko crumbs.
6. Pan fry for three minutes per side.

No-Bake Raspberry and Lavender Cake

Time: 3hrs **Serves:** 10

INGREDIENTS

- ½ cup oats
- 2 cups dates
- ½ cup dreed apricot
- ¼ cup peanuts
- 2tsp. cinnamon
- 8 bananas, mashed
- ½ cup coconut water
- ½ cup cashews
- 10 lavender leaves
- 4 dates
- ½ cup mixed berry

METHOD

1. Blend the two cups of dates, cinnamon, apricots, oats, and peanuts in a food processor.
2. Press into the base of your cake tin, and refrigerate.
3. Blitz half the banana, coconut water, cashews, and lavender leaves in your blender until it forms a paste.
4. Pour over the base, and freeze for an hour.
5. Blitz your bananas, berries, and dates until it forms a paste, then pour into the cake pan, and freeze for six hours.   Decorate with peanuts and lavender.

Whole-Wheat Zucchini Brownies

Time: 42mins **Serves:** 12

INGREDIENTS

- 1 cup whole wheat flour
- ½tbsp. ground flax seeds
- ½tsp. baking powder
- 1tsp. baking soda
- ¼tsp. ground cinnamon
- ½ cup sugar
- ¼tsp. salt
- ⅔ cup cocoa powder
- ½ cup brown sugar
- 1tsp. vanilla extract
- ⅓ cup margarine
- 1½ cups zucchini, shredded
- 2tbsp. dark chocolate chips
- ¼ cup chopped walnuts

METHOD

1. Preheat your oven to 350°F, and grease a 5x7 pan.   Combine the dry ingredients in one bowl, and cream the sugar with the margarine and vanilla in another.
2. Add the zucchini to the second mix, followed by the walnuts and chocolate chips. Mix this into the dry ingredients.   Bake for thirty to forty minutes. Allow to cool before cutting into squares.

Chocolate and Pumpkin Fudge Cake

Time: 50mins   **Serves:** 8

INGREDIENTS

- ½ cup water
- 3oz. vegan dark chocolate, melted
- ¾ cup pumpkin puree
- 2tsp. apple cider vinegar
- 2tsp. vanilla
- ½ cup packed brown sugar
- ¼ cup canola oil
- ¼ cup cocoa powder
- ½tsp. salt
- 1 cup all-purpose flour
- 1tsp. baking powder
- ½tsp. baking soda
- 1tsp. ground cinnamon
- ½tsp. ground allspice
- ½tsp. ground nutmeg
- ½tsp. ground cloves
- ⅛tsp. ground cayenne pepper
- ¼tsp. ground aniseed

METHOD

1. Preheat your oven to 350°F, and grease an 8-inch cake pan.
2. Combine the pumpkin, vinegar, water, sugar, vanilla, oil, and salt.
3. Sift together the flour, cocoa powder, baking soda, and baking powder, then stir in the spices.
4. Mix the twos together, then stir in the   melted chocolate.
5. Bake for 35 to 40 minutes.

Coffee and Cinnamon Cake

Time: 55mins   **Serves:** 9

INGREDIENTS

- ¾ cup sugar
- ½tsp. salt
- 1tbsp. baking powder
- ½ cup margarine
- 1tsp. cinnamon
- 2tbsp. sugar
- 2 cups flour
- ¼ cup soy yogurt
- 2tbsp. margarine
- ¾ cup milk

METHOD

1. Preheat your oven to 350°F, and grease a round cake pan
2. Combine the flour, baking powder, ¾-cup sugar, and salt.
3. Cut in the margarine.
4. To make the topped, take a half cup of this, and mix in the cinnamon and two tablespoons of sugar.
5. To the larger portion of dry ingredient, add the soy yogurt and milk and beat.
6. Pour into your pan, then spread the topping over.
7. Drizzle with two tablespoons melted margarine.
8. Bake for 35 minutes.

Death by Chocolate Mousse Cakes

Time: 2hrs 30mins   **Serves:** 3-4

INGREDIENTS

CRUST
- ¼tsp. baking powder
- ½ cup white flour
- ¼ cup brown sugar
- ¼ cup canola oil

MOUSSE
- 340g. firm silken tofu
- ½tsp. vanilla extract

CHOCOLATE SAUCE
- 1½tbsp. cocoa powder
- ½ cup sugar
- 1tbsp. white flour

- 3tbsp. cocoa powder
- 2tbsp. soymilk
- ¼tsp. salt
- 1tsp. vanilla extract

- 1 cup semisweet vegan chocolate chips
- ½ cup soymilk

- ½tsp. vanilla extract
- ½ cup soymilk

METHOD

1. To make the crust, preheat your oven to 350°F, and grease a muffin pan.
2. Combine the baking powder, flour, sugar, and cocoa powder.
3. In another bowl, mix the oil, soymilk, maple syrup, vanilla, and salt.
4. Combine the two mixtures, then divide between your muffin cups.
5. Bake for 10 to 18 minutes, then let cool.
6. To make the mousse, melt chocolate chips in microwave.
7. Blitz your melted chocolate chips, tofu, soymilk, and vanilla extract in a food processor.
8. Pour onto the crusts, and leave in the fridge for two hours.
9. To make the chocolate sauce, mix all the ingredients together in a small saucepan and bring to a boil. Take off the heat, leave to cool, then pour over your mousse cakes.

Lovely Lemon Drizzle Cake

Time: 1hr 10mins   **Serves:** 20-30

INGREDIENTS

- 1tsp. baking powder
- 1 large lemon
- ½tsp. salt
- ½ cup melted margarine
- 2 vegan egg substitute

- 1¾ cups flour
- 1 cup brown sugar
- ⅔ cup soymilk
- ¼ cup powdered sugar
- ½tsp. vanilla

METHOD

1. Preheat your oven to 350°F, and grease a loaf pan.
2. Combine all the dry ingredients but sugars.
3. Grate the lemon peel and add it to the mix.
4. In another bowl, squeeze the lemon juice and mix it with the powdered sugar. Reserve.
5. Beat the margarine, brown sugar, and egg replacer.
6. Combine the margarine mix with the dry mix, then add the vanilla.
7. Bake for an hour, the leave to cool for twenty minutes before turning out onto a rack.
8. Drizzle with the reserved lemon glaze.

Mug Cake

Time: 4mins   **Serves:** 1-2

INGREDIENTS

- 4tbsp. flour
- 2tbsp. dark cocoa
- 3tbsp. sugar
- 1 pinch salt
- 2tbsp. canola oil
- 1 pinch cinnamon
- 3tbsp. water
- chocolate chips
- 1tsp. vanilla

METHOD

1. Mix the dry ingredients in a microwave safe mug.
2. Stir in the liquids and chocolate chips until well combined.
3. Microwave on high for 60 seconds.

Low-Fat German Chocolate Cake

Time: 30mins   **Serves:** 10

INGREDIENTS

- ¾ cup pitted prune
- 2tbsp. egg replacer powder
- ½ cup water
- ½ cup water
- 2 cups unbleached all-purpose flour
- 2 cups sugar
- ¾ cup cocoa
- 1tsp. baking powder
- 2tsp. baking soda
- ½tsp. salt
- 2tsp. white vinegar
- 1 cup soymilk

METHOD

1. Preheat your oven to 350°F, and grease three 9-inch pans.
2. Chop the prunes in your food processor, then add the water until pureed.
3. Scrape the sides, then puree into a paste.
4. In another bowl, combine the Egg Replacer with water, mixing until smooth. Stir this into the prune puree until smooth and fluffy.
5. Add the sugar while beating.
6. Sift together the cocoa, flour, baking soda, baking powder, and salt.
7. Combine the soymilk and vinegar, and leave to sour for a few minutes.
8. Combine the flour mixture to the prune mixture, and add the soymilk, beating continuously until light and fluffly.   Divide between your pans, and bake for thirty minutes.

Walnut and Pumpkin Cake

Time: 50mins   **Serves:** 9

INGREDIENTS

- 1tsp. baking soda
- 1¾ cups cake flour
- 1tsp. ground cinnamon
- ¼tsp. nutmeg
- ¾tsp. ground ginger
- ½tsp. salt
- ¾ cup light brown sugar
- Egg replacer powder for 2 egg
- ½ cup vegetable oil
- 1 cup pumpkin puree
- ¾ cup granulated sugar
- ⅓ cup soymilk
- ¾ cup walnuts, chopped coarsely
- 1tsp. vanilla

METHOD

1. Preheat your oven to 350°F, and grease a 9-inch square baking pan.
2. Combine the baking soda, flour, cinnamon, nutmeg, ginger, and salt.
3. Beat the egg replacer and sugars until pale. Stir in the pumpkin, oil, milk, and vanilla.
4. Beat in the flour mixture until blended, then fold in the walnuts. Bake for around a half-hour.

Chocolate Death Cake

Time: 50mins   **Serves:** 10-12

INGREDIENTS

CAKE

- 4½ cups all-purpose flour
- 1 cup cocoa powder
- 3 cups sugar
- 1tbsp. baking soda
- 1½ cups vegetable oil
- 2tsp. salt
- 2tbsp. pure vanilla extract
- ¼ cup cider vinegar
- 3 cups strong brewed coffee

ICING

- 3 cups semisweet vegan chocolate chips
- 12oz. package firm silken tofu

METHOD

1. Preheat your oven to 350°F, and grease three 9-inch round cake pans.
2. Combine the dry ingredients, then add the oil and vanilla extract. Blend well.
3. Blend in the coffee while beating, then add the vinegar.
4. Divide between your pans, and bake for 20 to 25 minutes.   To make the icing, drain the fluid from silken tofu, then crush it and pop it into a saucepan with the chocolate chips.
5. Stir until the chocolate is very soft, then blitz in your food processor until smooth.
6. Cool, and spread between the layers of the cooled cake.

Sugar-Free Carrot Cake

Time: 1hr 30mins   **Serves:** 12

INGREDIENTS

- 1tsp. baking powder
- ¼tsp. salt
- 1tsp. baking soda
- 1¼ cups water
- 1 cup raisins
- 1 cup dates, chopped
- 1tsp. cinnamon
- ½tsp. ground cloves
- 2 cups whole wheat flour
- 1tsp. ground ginger
- ½tsp. ground nutmeg
- ⅓ cup frozen orange juice concentrate, thawed
- ½ cup carrot, grated

METHOD

1. Preheat your oven to 375°F, and grease a cake pan.
2. Combine the baking powder, flour, baking soda, and salt.   Combine the dates, water, raisins, ginger, cinnamon, cloves, and nutmeg in a saucepan, then bring to a boil and simmer for five minutes.
3. Pop the shredded carrot in a bowl, and pour the hot water mixture over them. Leave to cool completely.
4. Add the orange juice, and combine well.
5. Mix the two ingredients, and pour into your pan.   Bake for 45 minutes.

Chocolate Pudding Cake

Time: 1hr   **Serves:** 1

INGREDIENTS

- ⅔ cup sugar
- 1 cup flour
- 2tbsp. cocoa powder
- ⅛tsp. salt
- 2tsp. baking powder
- ½ cup water
- 1tsp. vanilla
- 2tsbp. applesauce
- ¼ cup cocoa
- 13/4 cups hot water
- ⅔ cup brown sugar

METHOD

1. Preheat your oven to 350°F, and grease an 8" square pan/dish.
2. Combine all the ingredients bar the last three. Pour into the pan.
3. Mix the cocoa and brown sugar, then sprinkle over the mix in pan.
4. Pour the hot water over everything. Bake for 45 minutes.

Gluten-Free Apple and Chocolate Cake

Time: 50mins   **Serves:** 12

INGREDIENTS

- ¼ cup potato starch
- ¼ cup unsweetened cocoa powder
- ¼ cup tapioca starch
- ½tsp. baking powder
- ¼tsp. xanthan gum
- ½tsp. baking soda
- ⅔ cup erythritol
- 1 cup brown rice flour
- 1tsp. lemon juice
- ¼ cup unsweetened applesauce
- 2tbsp. olive oil
- ¼tsp. allspice
- 1tsp. cinnamon
- 1tsp. vanilla
- 1 cup water
- 1 large apple

METHOD

1. Preheat your oven to 350°F, and grease a 9-inch' round pan.
2. Combine the baking powder, flours, soda, cocoa powder, xanthan, cinnamon, and allspice.

Combine the water, applesauce, oil, vanilla, lemon juice, and erythritol. Peel and core apple, then chop into small pieces and add to wet mixture. Combine the two mixtures, then bake for thirty to forty minutes.

Bubble and Squeak

Time: 40mins   **Serves:** 8

INGREDIENTS

- 2lbs potatoes, peeled, quartered, and boiled until tender
- 14-17oz. Brussels sprouts, ends chopped off and cooked
- 4tbsp. Earth Balance margarine
- ½ cup all-purpose flour
- oil (for frying)
- Old Bay Seasoning

METHOD

1. Finely shred the cooked sprouts.   Mash the potatoes with the Earth Balance, then mix in the sprouts with a quarter-teaspoons of Old Bay seasoning. Shape into patties.
2. Mix the cup flour with a half-teaspoon of Old Bay, and preheat the oil in a skillet over a medium heat.
3. Coat each patty in the flour mixture, then fry for two to three minutes per side.
4. Preheat your oven to 375° F, and line a baking sheet with parchment paper.
5. Lay your fried patties on the sheet, then bake for fifteen minutes, until crisp.

Three Milk Cake

Time: 1hr   **Serves:** 8

INGREDIENTS

- 1¾ cups pastry flour
- 1tsp. baking soda
- 1tsp. baking powder
- ½tsp. salt
- 1 cup vegan sugar
- ⅓ cup Earth Balance whipped spread
- ⅔ cup filtered water
- 1tbsp. cider vinegar
- 2tsp. real vanilla extract

MILK MIXTURE

- 2tbsp. coconut milk
- 2tbsp. cream of coconut
- 2 cups plain soymilk
- 2tsp. lime juice
- 2 cups vegan whipped topping

METHOD

1. Preheat your oven to 350°F, and grease an 8-inch cake pan.   Combine the flour, baking powder, and baking soda. Beat together the salt, sugar, margarine, water, vanilla, and vinegar.
2. Combine the two mixtures, and bake for thirty to forty minutes.
3. Cool completely, then cut in half horizontally to form two layers.
4. To make the frosting, mix the cream of coconut and coconut milk together, then pour into a saucepan.

Beat in the soymilk, lime juice, and whipping cream until smooth. Bring mixture to a full boil, stirring often.

5. Pour the hot milk over the bottom layer of cake, and press with a spatula until all the milk has been absorbed. Replace the top layer of the cake, and pour more milk over the top.
6. Let soak in the fridge for thirty minutes.

Spiced Walnut Cake

Time: 1hr   **Serves:** 20

INGREDIENTS

- 1tsp. baking soda
- 2½ cups all-purpose flour
- ½tsp. ground cloves
- ¾tsp. ground nutmeg

- 1tsp. ground cinnamon
- ¾tsp. salt
- 1 cup packed light brown sugar
- 1 cup granulated sugar

- ¾ cup vegetable shortening
- 1¼ cups soymilk
- 1 cup applesauce

FROSTING

- ½ cup vegan margarine
- ½tsp. rum extract
- 1tsp. maple extract

- 2x16oz. boxes confectioners' sugar
- ½ cup vegetable shortening

- 1½ cups walnuts, toasted, chopped coarsely
- 6-8 teaspoons soymilk

METHOD

1. Preheat your oven to 350°F, and grease two 9-inch cake pans.
2. Combine the flour, clove, baking soda, cinnamon, nutmeg, and salt.
3. Combine the sugars, applesauce, and shortening, then combine this with the first mixture. Add the soymilk, and beat some more.
4. Divide between your pans, and bake for 35 minutes.
5. To make the frosting, beat the shortening, margarine, and extracts. Slowly beat in confectioner's sugar and the soymilk/water.
6. Wait until the cake is completely cooled before spreading.

Applesauce and Chocolate Cake

Time: 1hr 5mins**Serves:** 10

INGREDIENTS

- 1 cup sugar
- 2tsp. baking soda
- 1tbsp. cornstarch

- 2 cups flour
- ¼tsp. salt
- 1½ cups applesauce

- ⅓ cup cocoa

METHOD

1. Preheat your oven to 325°F, and grease a Bundt pan.
2. Combine all the ingredients well.   Bake for 50 to 55 minutes.

Chocolate and ZucchiniCake

Time: 1hr

INGREDIENTS

- 1½ cups zucchini, peeled and grated
- ¼ cup canola oil
- 1 ripe banana, mashed
- 1⅓ cups whole wheat

- pastry flour
- 1tbsp. stevia
- 1 cup applesauce
- 1tsp. salt
- 1tsp. cinnamon

- 1tsp. baking soda
- 1tsp. vanilla
- ½ cup semi-sweet chocolate chips
- ¼ cup ground walnuts

METHOD

1. Preheat your oven to 350°F, and grease a pan.
2. Mix all the dry ingredients in one bowl, and all the wet ingredients in another.
3. Mix the two together, then fold in the chocolate chips.   Bake for 45-60 minutes.

Apple and Coffee Cake

Time: 1hr 30mins   **Serves:** 15-25

INGREDIENTS

- 2tbsp. cinnamon
- 5-6 cups apples, peeled and sliced
- 5tbsp. sugar
- 2 cups sugar
- 4tsp. vanilla
- 1 cup applesauce
- ½ cup orange juice
- 4 egg substitute
- 1 pinch salt
- 3 cups flour
- 1tsp. nutmeg
- 1tbsp. baking powder

METHOD

1. Preheat your oven to 350°F, and grease a Bundt pan.
2. Combine the sugar and cinnamon and use this to coat the apple, reserving a tablespoon of the sugar mix for later.
3. Beat the applesauce, sugar, vanilla, orange juice, salt, and egg replacers.
4. Fold in the baking powder, flour, and nutmeg.
5. Spoon half into your pan, then cover with half the apple mixture.
6. Cover with half of the apple mixture.
7. Repeat, then sprinkle with the reserved cinnamon-sugar.
8. Bake for around an hour, then let cool before turning out onto a plate.

Vanilla Cake with Strawberry, Walnut, and Coconut Frosting

Time: 50mins   **Serves:** 8

INGREDIENTS

- 1 cup sugar
- 13⁄4 cups all-purpose flour
- ¼tsp. salt
  FROSTING
- 2 cups powdered sugar
- 2tbsp. soymilk
- 11⁄2tbsp. vegan butter
- 2tsp. vanilla extract
- 1 cup soymilk
- ⅓ cup olive oil

- 1tsp. vanilla extract
- 3⁄4 cup walnuts
- 3 cups fresh strawberries
- 2tbsp. coconut oil
- 1tbsp. lemon juice

- ¼ cup shredded coconut

METHOD

1. Preheat your oven to 350°F, and grease a cake pan.
2. Sift together the flour, sugar, and salt. Stir in the soymilk, vanilla, and olive oil.
3. Bake for around thirty minutes and leave to cool.

To make the frosting, beat together the sugar, butter, and soymilk until creamy.

Once the cake is cool, spread with the frosting, then sprinkle on the coconut, walnuts, and strawberries.

Luxurious Lemon Cake

Time: 40mins   **Serves:** 12

INGREDIENTS

- 200g. caster sugar
- 1 lemon zest and juice
- 1tsp. baking powder
- 100ml. vegetable oil
- 275g. self-rising flour
- 150g. confectioners' sugar
- 170ml. cold water

METHOD

1. Preheat your oven to 200°C, and grease a cake pan.
2. Combine all your ingredients well, then bake for around thirty minutes.

Six-Ingredient Mug Cake

Time: 5mins

INGREDIENTS

- 3½tbsp. chai tea mix
- 3½tbsp. whole wheat flour
- 35g. bittersweet chocolate
- ⅛tsp. baking powder
- ½tbsp. chocolate chips
- ⅛tsp. baking soda

METHOD

1. Take your mug, and mix the tea with the chocolate, then melt it in the microwave.
2. Stir in the flour using a fork, followed by the baking powder and soda, then the chocolate chips.
3. Microwave for a further minutes.

Pumpkin and Walnut Cake

Time: 45mins   **Serves:** 16

INGREDIENTS

- 200g. brown sugar
- 100g. vegan butter
- 120g. white sugar
- Egg replacer powder for 2 egg
- 1tsp. vanilla extract
- 100g. soymilk
- 200g. pumpkin puree
- 1tsp. baking soda
- 250g. flour
- ½tsp. salt
- 1tsp. ground ginger
- 1tsp. cinnamon
- ½tsp. nutmeg
- 50g. walnuts, coarsely chopped
- ¼tsp. mace

METHOD

1. Preheat your oven to 350°F, and grease a 9-inch square cake pan.
2. Cream the butter with the sugar, then add the egg replacer, vanilla, soymilk, and pumpkin.
3. Add the flour, salt, baking soda, cinnamon, nutmeg, ginger, and cloves.
4. Fold in the walnuts, then back for 30-35 minutes.

Beautiful Banana Cake

Time: 1hr 20mins   **Serves:** 8-10

INGREDIENTS

- 1½tsp. baking soda
- ¼ cup water
- ½tsp. salt
- 1tsp. vanilla
- ½ cup powdered sugar
- 1tbsp. egg substitute
- 2 cups flour
- ½ cup brown sugar, packed
- 5 bananas, mashed
- ¼ cup oil
- water, as needed
- 1 cup chocolate chips
- ½ cup walnuts, chopped

METHOD

1. Preheat your oven to 350°F, and grease a 9-inch square pan.
2. Combine your baking soda, flour, and salt.
3. In another bowl, beat a quarter-cup of water with the vanilla and the egg replacer until it forms soft peaks.
4. Slowly add the sugar, beat continuously.
5. Add the remaining ingredients and mix well, then fold in the walnuts and chocolate chips.
6. Bake for around fifty minutes.

Pumpkin Bundt Cake

Time: 1hr 5mins   **Serves:** 10

INGREDIENTS

- 1 cup all-purpose flour
- 1¼ cups whole wheat flour
- 2tsp. baking powder
- 1½tsp. cinnamon
- 1tsp. baking soda
- 1tsp. allspice
- 1¼ cups canned pumpkin
- ½tsp. salt
- 2½tsp. lemon juice
- 1tsp. vanilla
- ¾ cup soymilk
- 1 cup unsalted butter, softened
- 3tbsp. Ener-G Egg Substitute
- 1¼ cups granulated sugar

METHOD

1. Preheat your oven to 350°F, and grease your Bundt pan.
2. Mix your soymilk and lemon juice and leave to sour.
3. Beat together all the ingredients until smooth and combined.
4. Bake for 45 to 50 minutes.

Maple Turtle Cake

Time: 3hrs

INGREDIENTS

CAKE

- ⅓ cup unsweetened cocoa powder
- 1tsp. salt
- 1tsp. baking soda

SALTED MAPLE CARAMEL

- ½ cup water
- 2 cups maple sugar
- ¼ cup light agave nectar

FROSTING

- 2tbsp. coconut oil
- 1½ cups agave nectar
- 1tbsp. coconut milk

- 1 cup maple sugar
- 1 cup coconut milk
- 1½ cups whole wheat pastry flour

- 2tbsp. Earth Balance natural buttery spread
- ½ cup full fat coconut milk

- ¾tsp. salt
- 1½ cups sifted cocoa powder

- ½ cup coconut oil
- 1tbsp. maple extract
- 2tbsp. cider vinegar
- 1tbsp. pure vanilla extract

- 1tbsp. pure vanilla extract
- 2tsp. salt
- 1tbsp. maple extract

- 1tbsp. pure vanilla extract
- 2½ cups toasted pecans
- 2tsp. maple extract

METHOD

1. Preheat your oven to 375°F, and grease two six-inch cake pans.
2. Beat together all the cake ingredients, then divide between the cake pans.
3. Bake for around a half-hour, then leave to cool completely in the pan.
4. Refrigerate until very cold, then slice three times horizontally, to create four thin cakes.
5. To make the caramel, pop the sugar, agave nectar, and water in a saucepan over medium-high heat, and bring to a boil, stirring well until the sugar dissolves.
6. Turn down the heat and cook without stirring until the liquid is deep amber in color, about fifteen to twenty minutes.
7. Remove from the heat, then carefully stir in the coconut milk, earth balance butter, vanilla, maple extract, and salt until smooth.
8. To make the frosting, beat all the ingredients until smooth.
9. To build your cake, layer in the following order: cake, frosting, toasted pecans, caramel, cake. Repeat until you end with frosting and a scattering of the pecans.

Gluten-Fruit Double Chocolate Cake

Time: 40mins   **Serves:** 4-6

INGREDIENTS

- ½ cup brown sugar
- 1 cup applesauce
- 1tsp. vanilla
- ½tsp. xanthan gum
- ¾ cup gluten-free flour
- ⅓ cup cocoa
- ½tsp. baking soda
- 2tsp. baking powder
- ½tsp. salt
- ½ cup chocolate chips
- 1 pinch cinnamon

METHOD

Preheat your oven to 350°F, and grease an 8x8-inch square pan. Beat all your ingredients together until well-combined, then fold in the chocolate chips.   Bake for around half an hour.

Kjøttkaker: Norwegian Lentil Cakes With Gravy

Time: 1hr 15mins   **Serves:** 4

INGREDIENTS

- 1½tsp. salt
- ¼tsp. ground nutmeg
- ¼tsp. pepper
  GRAVY
- 2-3tbsp. cornstarch
- 2tbsp. onions, finely chopped
- 1 cup lentils
- ¼tsp. ground ginger
- ¾ cup plain unsweetened

- soymilk
- 2½tbsp. cornstarch

- 2 cups plain unsweetened soymilk
- Salt and pepper, to taste

METHOD

1. Simmer the lentils for thirty minutes, until softened. Drain well.
2. Chuck your lentils in the food processor, along with the salt, pepper, ginger, nutmeg, and cornstarch.
3. Scrape into a bowl, then gradually add the soymilk.
4. Shape into patties, then fry in Earth Balance in a skillet, for six to seven minutes per side.
5. Bring the gravy soymilk to a boil, then reduce to a low simmer. Add your cooked patties, and simmer for ten to fifteen minutes, then remove with a slotted spoon and reserve.
6. To finish the gravy, blend a tablespoon or two of cornstarch with a little cold water, stir it into the cooking soymilk to thicken. Add the onion, season well, and cook until thickened.

Carrot Cake with a Cashew and Strawberry Cream Frosting

Time: 50mins   **Serves:** 12

INGREDIENTS

- 1 cup whole wheat pastry flour
- 1tsp. baking powder
- ½ cup barley flour
- 1tsp. baking soda
  FROSTING
- 3 dates
- 7 strawberries
- ½tbsp. coconut oil
- ¼tsp. salt
- 1tsp. cinnamon
- 2 cups carrots, shredded
- 1 cup applesauce

- 1tsp. vanilla extract
- ¾ cup cashews
- ½tbsp. lemon zest
- ½ cup safflower oil
- ¼ cup sugar
- ¼ cup maple sugar
- 1tsp. vanilla

- ⅛ cup lemon juice

METHOD

1. Preheat your oven to 365°F, and grease two round 9-inch cake pans.
2. Combine the dry ingredients.   Combine the wet ingredients.
3. Combine the two, then fold in the carrots.   Divide between your pans, and bake for 35-40 minutes.
4. To make the frosting, soak the cashews in a cup of fresh water for 30 minutes, then drain and rinse.
5. Soak the dates in a cup of water for fifteen minutes, but reserve the water. Put all the frosting ingredients in your food processor and blend until smooth. Only add the date water if needed.

Gluten-Free, Sugar-Free Chocolate Cake With Frosting

Time: 45mins   **Serves:** 8

INGREDIENTS

CUP

- 2 cups brown rice flour
- 3/4 cup unsweetened cocoa powder
- 1/2 cup tapioca flour
- 1½tsp. baking soda

FROSTING

- 2 cups palm shortening
- 1 cup agave nectar

- 1/2tsp. salt
- 1½tsp. xanthan gum
- 1½ cups boiling water
- 1/2 cup virgin coconut oil

- 1 cup arrowroot
- 4tsp. vanilla

- 1 cup prune
- 1 cup maple syrup
- 1tbsp. vanilla
- 2tbsp. apple cider vinegar

- 2-4tsp. beet juice
- 2tsp. almond flavoring

METHOD

1. Preheat your oven to 350°F, and grease two 9-inch cake pans.
2. Soak the prunes in boiling water for ten minutes.
3. Combine the brown rice flour, cocoa powder, tapioca flour, baking soda, xanthan gum, and salt.
4. Pop the prunes, along with the water, into your food processor, then add the coconut oil, water, maple syrup, apple cider vinegar, and vanilla. Blend until smooth, then pour into your dry mix and gently combine.
5. Divide between your pans, and bake for 25 minutes.
6. To make the frosting, beat all the ingredients together well, then spread on the cake once cooled.

Raw German Chocolate Coconut Cake

Time: 45mins   **Serves:** 8

INGREDIENTS

- 20oz. dates, blended to a paste
- 3/4 cup extra virgin

- coconut oil
- 1/2tsp. salt
- 4tbsp. vanilla

WALNUT AND COCONUT FILLING

- 1 cup agave syrup
- 5 cups chopped walnuts

CHOCOLATE FROSTING

- 1/2 cup cacao, nibs
- 3/4 cup almond milk
- 1½oz. cacao, powder

(set aside 1 cup)

- 2tbsp. vanilla

- 3oz. dates, paste
- 1/2 cup agave syrup
- 4tbsp. vanilla

- 7-9 cups almond flour
- 1/2 cup coconut milk
- 2½oz. cacao, powder

- 3 cups coconut flakes
- 1/4tsp. salt

- 2tsp. extra virgin coconut oil
- 1/4tsp. salt

METHOD

Combine all the ingredients until smooth, then divide between two eight-inch cake pans. Pop into the freezer.

To make the filling, blitz four cups of walnuts, the agave, vanilla, and salt in your food processor until smooth. Fold in the rest of the walnuts and the coconut flakes.

Fill the cakes, then return to the freezer.

To make the frosting, blitz all the ingredients in the blender until smooth, then leave in the fridge until thickened.

Carrot and Ginger Cake

Time: 1hr 15mins   **Serves:** 12

INGREDIENTS

- 1⁄4 cup safflower oil
- 1⁄3 cup maple syrup
- 1⁄3 cup raisins
- 4-5tbsp. unsweetened applesauce
- 3 medium carrots, grated
- 1 orange, zest of
- 2tsp. fresh gingerroot, finely grated
- 1½tsp. baking powder
- 2 cups whole wheat pastry flour
- 3⁄4 cup apple juice
- 1¼tsp. baking soda
- 1⁄2tsp. nutmeg
- 1-1½tsp. cinnamon
- 1⁄2tsp. salt
- 1 cup walnuts
- 2⁄3 cup raisins

METHOD

1. Preheat your oven to 350°F, and grease an 8x8 pan.
2. Combine all the ingredients but the carrots, raisins, and walnuts. Mix well.
3. Fold in the rest of the ingredients, then pour into the pan.   Bake for 35 to 45 minutes.

Red Velvet Cake with a Cream Cheese Frosting

Time: 1hr   **Serves:** 10

INGREDIENTS

- 1½ cups turbinado
- 8tbsp. margarine
- 1⁄2 cup unsweetened applesauce
- 1 cup soymilk
- 2tbsp. unsweetened cocoa powder
- 1tbsp. lemon juice
- 1½tsp. baking soda
- 2½ cups unbleached flour
- 1tsp. vanilla extract
- 1tsp. vinegar
- 1tsp. salt
- 2oz. vegan red food coloring
- 8oz. cream cheese
- 1 cup confectioners' sugar
- 8tbsp. margarine
- 1⁄2-1 cup vanilla soymilk
- 1tsp. vanilla

METHOD

1. Preheat oven to 350°F, and grease two cake pans.
2. Mix the milk with the lemon juice, and leave to sour.
3. Cream together the margarine and sugar, then stir in the applesauce and flour.
4. Combine the cocoa and food coloring, then add it to the creamed mixture.
5. Mix in the rest of the ingredients, then divide between your tins, and bake for forty minutes.
6. To make the frosting, combine the ingredients all together, then spread over the cakes when cooled completely.

Coconut and Pecan Cake

Time: 40mins   **Serves:** 6

INGREDIENTS

- 3⁄4 cup of semolina flour
- 3⁄4 cup turbinado sugar
- 1⁄2 cup all-purpose flour
- 1tsp. baking powder
- 1⁄4 cup canola oil
- 1⁄2tsp. salt
- 1⁄4 cup applesauce
- 1⁄2tsp. orange blossom water
- 3⁄4tsp. vanilla
- 3⁄4 cup of organic soymilk
- 1⁄2 cup almonds
- 1⁄4 cup sweetened flaked coconut

METHOD

1. Preheat your oven to 350°F, and grease a pie pan.   Combine the dry ingredients thoroughly.
2. Mix in the oil, extracts, applesauce, milk, and coconut.   Bake for 30 minutes.

Lemon Loaf

Time: 1hr 15mins   **Serves:** 8-10

INGREDIENTS

- 1½ cups brown sugar
- 1 cup canola oil
- 4 Ener-G eggs
- ½tsp. salt
- 2tbsp. lemon zest
- 2tsp. baking powder
- 1 cup unsweetened soymilk
- 3 cups unbleached all-purpose flour

METHOD

1. Preheat your oven to 335°F, and grease a loaf pan.
2. Mix together the oil, lemon zest, sugar, and the pre-mixed Ener-G Eggs.
3. Stir in the baking soda, flour, salt, and milk until smooth.
4. Bake for around an hour, until cracked and peaked on top.

Carrot and Raisin Cake!

Time: 1hr 30mins   **Serves:** 25-30

INGREDIENTS

- 1½ cups raisins
- 2 cups carrots, finely grated
- 2 cups water
- 1½ bananas, mashed
- 2 Egg substitute
- 1 cup silken tofu
- ¼ maple syrup
- 3tbsp. soy yogurt
- 3½tbsp. extra virgin olive oil
- 3½tbsp. applesauce (unsweetened)
- ½ cup agave syrup
- 1½tsp. allspice
- ½tsp. ground cloves
- 1½tsp. cinnamon
- 1tsp. ground ginger
- 3 cups spelt flour
- 2tsp. salt
- 2tsp. baking soda
- 8tbsp. flaxseed meal
- ¾ cup walnuts. chopped

METHOD

1. Preheat your oven to 350°F, and grease three 9-inch pans.
2. Simmer the carrots and raisins in water for seven to ten minutes.
3. Combine the applesauce, oil, spices, syrups, egg replacer, and salt.
4. Mix in the carrot and raisins.   Stir together the flour, flaxseed meal, nuts, and baking soda.
5. Combine the dries to the wets, then divide between your pans.
6. Bake for thirty minutes, then reduce the heat to 300°F and cook for another fifteen minutes.

Peanut Butter and Chocolate Chip Cake

Time: 35mins   **Serves:** 9

INGREDIENTS

- 1 cup whole wheat pastry flour
- 1tbsp. oil, to grease
- ⅓ cup sugar
- 1½tsp. baking powder
- ½tsp. salt
- ½ cup soymilk
- ½ cup applesauce
- ½ cup peanut butter
- ⅓ cup almonds, chopped
- 1 cup semi-sweet chocolate chips

METHOD

1. Preheat your oven to 350°F, and grease a 9-inch cake pan.
2. Mix together the baking powder, flour, sugar, and salt.
3. Stir together the non-dairy milk, applesauce, and peanut butter in another bowl until smooth.
4. Combine the two mixtures until smooth.
5. Fold in the chocolate chips, then bake for 25 to 30 minutes.

Charlie's Chocolate Cake

Time: 55mins   **Serves:** 6-8

INGREDIENTS

- 2½ cups flour
- 1⅓ cups sugar
- 3⁄4 cup cocoa
- 2tsp. baking soda
- 1⁄4 cup oil
- ½tsp. salt
- 1⁄4 cup applesauce
- 1⁄4 cup vinegar
- 2⅓ cups water

METHOD

1. Preheat your oven to 350°F, and grease a 9x9 pan.
2. Combine everything well, then bake for around fifty minutes.

Gooey Tasty Cocolate Cake

Time: 45mins   **Serves:** 1

INGREDIENTS

- 1½ cups all-purpose flour
- 1tsp. baking soda
- 3tbsp. cocoa
- 1 cup white sugar
- 5tbsp. canola oil
- ½tsp. salt
- 1tbsp. white vinegar
- 1 cup cold water
- 1tsp. vanilla extract

METHOD

1. Preheat your oven to 350°F, and grease a 9x9 inch pan.
2. Mix your flour with the cocoa, sugar, baking soda, and salt.
3. Add the oil, vinegar, and vanilla, then the water.
4. Mix it all together well, then pour into the pan and bake for around thirty minutes.

Tofu Pound Cake

Time: 1hr 10mins   **Serves:** 8

INGREDIENTS

- 1½ cups unbleached cane sugar
- 1½tsp. lemon extract
- 1tsp. baking powder
- 3⁄4 cup low-fat silken tofu
- ½ cup softened vegan margarine
- 2 cups white spelt flour
- ½ cup water

METHOD

1. Preheat your oven to 350'F, and grease a load pan.
2. Combine the ingredients until smooth.
3. Bake for around fifty minutes.

Iced Burnt Sugar Cake

Time: 1hr 5mins   **Serves:** 8-10

INGREDIENTS
CAKE
- ½ cup margarine (Earth Balance)
- 3tsp. egg substitute
- 1½ cups sugar
ICING
- 2 cups sugar
- ½ cup vegan cream
- ½ cup margarine (Earth Balance)

- 4tbsp. filtered water
- 2½ cups flour
- 1 cup water

- 4tbsp. burnt sugar syrup
- 2tsp. baking powder
- 1tsp. vanilla extract

- ¼ cup agave nectar
- Remaining burnt sugar syrup
- 1tsp. vanilla

METHOD
1. Preheat your oven to 350°F, and grease a 9x13 pan.
2. To make the cake, cream the margarine with the sugar.
3. Stir in the egg replacer, vanilla, water, and burnt sugar syrup.
4. Mix in the flour and baking powder. Bake for 35 minutes, then leave to cool.
5. To make the icing, combine the ingredients in a saucepan and heat gently.
6. Pour over the cake, and leave it to cool.

Low-Fat, Low-Sugar Chocolate Cake

Time: 30mins   **Serves:** 8

INGREDIENTS
- ⅓ cup cocoa powder
- 1 cup flour
- 1 cup banana, mashed
FILLIING
- 1tbsp. raspberry jam

- 1tbsp. maple syrup
- ½ cup pineapple juice
- 1 pinch salt

- 100ml. soy yogurt

- 2tsp. vinegar
- 1tsp. baking soda

METHOD
1. Preheat your oven to 190°C, and grease a loaf pan.   Combine the dry ingredients together.
2. Stir in the banana, maple syrup, pineapple juice, and salt.
3. Stir in the vinegar until it begins to froth, then bake for twenty minutes.
4. Turn out onto a wire rack and leave to cool.
5. Slice the cake horizontally. Spread both halves with yoghurt, then add jam, and sandwich.

Low-Fat Carrot Cake

Time: 1hr 20mins   **Serves:** 12

INGREDIENTS
- 2tsp. baking soda
- 2 cups whole wheat pastry flour
- 2tsp. baking powder

- 1tsp. salt
- 1tbsp. cinnamon
- 2 cups carrots, grated
- 2 cups applesauce

- 1 cup soymilk
- ½ cup maple syrup
- ½ cup crushed walnuts
- 2tbsp. stevia

METHOD
1. Preheat your oven to 350°F, and grease a 13x9 pan.
2. Combine the flour, baking powder, baking soda, cinnamon, stevia, and salt.
3. Add the carrots and all the wet ingredients until mixed, then fold in the walnuts.
4. Cook for around 45 minutes.

Truly Chocolatey Chocolate Cake

Time: 1hr   **Serves:** 8

INGREDIENTS

CAKE

- 1½ cups unbleached white flour
- ½tsp. baking soda
- ⅓ cup unsweetened cocoa powder
- ½tsp. salt
- ½ cup vegetable oil
- 1 cup sugar
- 1 cup chilled brewed coffee
- 2tbsp. cider vinegar
- 2tsp. pure vanilla extract

RASPBERRY GLAZE

- 1½ cups dark chocolate chips
- 2tsp. water
- ⅓ cup raspberry jam
- 2 cups raspberry jam

METHOD

1. Preheat your oven to 375°F, and grease an 8-inch baking pan.
2. Combine the flour, baking soda, cocoa, salt, and sugar. Mix together the oil, coffee, and vanilla.
3. Blend the two mixtures together, then add the vinegar until it froths.
4. Bake for around thirty minutes.
5. To make the glaze, melt a third-cup of jam and chocolate together well.
6. In another small saucepan, mix two cups of jam with two teaspoons of water, then brush this all over the cooled cake.   Spread the chocolate and jam mixture over this.

Awesome Apple Cake

Time: 1hr 25mins   **Serves:** 8

INGREDIENTS

- 400g. no-added-sugar apple pie filling
- 120g. margarine, melted
- 1 cup brown sugar
- 2tbsp. unsweetened cocoa
- 2 cups plain flour
- 2tsp. baking powder
- 1tsp. mixed spice
- 1tsp. baking soda

METHOD

1. Preheat your oven to 325°F, and grease a pan.
2. Combine the dry ingredients, then stir in the apple and melted margarine.
3. Bake until a skewer inserted into the middle of the cake comes out clean.

Coffee and Pineapple Cake

Time: 55mins   **Serves:** 7-9

INGREDIENTS

- 1 cup quick oats
- ½ cup sugar
- 1 cup whole wheat flour
- 2tsp. baking powder
- ½tsp. ground cinnamon

TOPPING

- ½tsp. cinnamon
- 1½tsp. Ener-G Egg Substitute
- ½tsp. baking soda
- 3tbsp. water
- ½tsp. salt
- 1tbsp. white vinegar
- ⅓ cup unsweetened applesauce
- 1 cup crushed pineapple in juice, undrained
- 2tbsp. coarse sugar

METHOD

1. Preheat your the oven to 350°F, and grease an 8x8 inch glass baking pan.
2. Blitz your oats in a blender and grind until they are fine.
3. Combine with the other dry ingredients, then add the wet ingredients and gently mix.
4. Pour into the pan, then sprinkle on the sugar and cinnamon topping. Bake for thirty to forty minutes.

Coffee Cake

Time: 40mins   **Serves:** 6-8

INGREDIENTS

- 2¼ cups flour
- 2tsp. cinnamon
- ½tsp. salt
- ¼tsp. ground ginger
- ¾ cup unbleached cane

- sugar
- ¾ cup brown sugar
- ¾ cup canola oil
- 1tsp. baking soda
- 1 cup walnuts

- 1tsp. baking powder
- 1 cup soymilk, with 3tsp. lemon juice
- 2tsp. egg substitute, with 2tbsp. water

METHOD

1. Preheat your oven to 350°F, and grease a 9x13 baking pan.
2. Combine the flour, half the cinnamon, salt, ginger, both sugars, and oil. Remove a ¾ cup of that mixture, then add the rest of the cinnamon and the nuts. Reserve. This is the topping.
3. To the remaining flour mixture, add baking soda, egg-replacer mixture, baking powder, and milk.
4. Pour the batter into the dish, then cover with the topping.   Bake for 35 to 45 minutes.

Raspberry Choca-Mocha Cake

Time: 50mins   **Serves:** 4

INGREDIENTS

- 1½ cups sugar
- ½ cup cocoa
- 2tsp. baking soda
- ¼ cup oil

- 2tsp. vinegar, dissolved in ¼ cup water
- 3 cups flour
- 1½tsp. vanilla

- ¾ cup strong brewed coffee
- chocolate frosting
- ¾ cup raspberry preserves

METHOD

1. Preheat your oven to 350°F, and grease a cake pan.
2. Combine the flour, baking soda, sugar, and cocoa. Add the oil and vanilla, followed by the vinegar and water, and finally the coffee and raspberry preserves.
3. Beat until smooth, then bake for 25 minutes.   Cool completely before topping with the frosting.

Coffee and Chocolate Layer Cake

Time: 45mins   **Serves:** 12

INGREDIENTS

- 1 cup maple syrup
- 2tsp. vanilla extract
- ¾ cup strong black coffee, brewed and cold
- 1 cup unsweetened cocoa
  FROSTING
- 10½oz. tofu, extra-firm silken
- 6oz. semisweet chocolate chips, melted

- powder
- ½ cup all-purpose flour
- ¾ cup whole wheat pastry flour
- 1tsp. baking powder

- 1 cup low-fat firm silken tofu, pureed
- ½tsp. ground cinnamon
- 1tsp. baking soda

- 2tsp. vanilla extract

METHOD

1. Preheat your oven to 350°F, and grease two 8-inch cake pans.
2. Beat together the tofu, coffee, syrup, a quarter-cup of water, and vanilla.
3. Sift together the rest of the cake ingredients.   Blend the two mixtures, and whisk together well.
4. Divide between the pans and bake for fifteen minutes.
5. Cool for ten minutes before removing from the pan.
6. To make the frosting, blitz your tofu, vanilla, and chocolate in your food processor.
7. Fill the cake when cool, and garnish with raspberries.

Vegan Cookies

Chewy Chocolate Chip Cookies

Time: 35mins   **Serves:** 9

INGREDIENTS

- 2 cups sugar
- 1tbsp. flaxseed, plus 1tsp. flaxseed
- 2tsp. vanilla
- ½ cup soymilk
- ¾ cup canola oil
- ¾ cup cocoa powder
- 2 cups flour
- 1tsp. baking soda
- 1½ cups semisweet chocolate chips
- ½tsp. salt

METHOD

1. Preheat your oven to 350°F, and line a cookie sheet.
2. Grind the flaxseeds in a food processor until they become a fine powder, then add the soymilk and blend for about thirty seconds more. Sift the cocoa with the flour, baking soda, and salt.
3. Cream together the sugar and oil, then stir in the flaxseed and soymilk.
4. Add the vanilla, then mix in the dry ingredients. . Mix in the chocolate chips.
5. Roll the dough into 1-inch balls and flatten into disks of about 1.5-inches in diameter.
6. Bake for around ten minutes, then leave to cool for five minutes before removing them from the sheet.

Ginger Cookies

TIME: 40mins

INGREDIENTS

- 4tbsp. coarse sugar
- 1tsp. baking soda
- 2 cups flour
- ¼tsp. salt
- ½tsp. ground cinnamon
- 2½tbsp. ground ginger
- ½tsp. ground cloves
- ¼ cup molasses
- ½ cup canola oil
- ¼ cup soymilk
- 1tsp. vanilla
- 1 cup sugar

METHOD

1. Preheat your oven to 350°F, and grease a cookie sheet.
2. Combine the wet ingredients with the sugar.   Sift together the remaining dry ingredients.
3. Blend them together, then roll into small balls and flatten onto your cookie sheet. Sprinkle with coarse sugar, then bake for ten minutes.

Oaty Banana Cookies

TIME: 33mins   **SERVES:** 36

INGREDIENTS

- ⅓ cup oil, plus
- ½ cup sugar
- 1tsp. oil
- 1½tsp. vanilla extract
- 1 banana, mashed
- 1½ cups flour
- 1½tsp. cinnamon
- 1 cup brown sugar
- 1tsp. baking soda
- ½tsp. salt
- 3tbsp. water
- 2¼ cups oats

METHOD

1. Preheat your oven to 350°F, and grease a cookie sheet.
2. Combine the baking soda, flour, cinnamon, and salt. Combine the brown sugar, oil, sugar, and water.
3. Stir in the banana and vanilla, followed by the flour mixture.
4. Stir in the oats, then drop tablespoons of the mix onto your cookie sheet. Bake for thirteen minutes.

Lemon Cookies

TIME: 20mins   **SERVES:** 20

INGREDIENTS

- 1½ cups sugar
- 2½ cups flour
- 2tsp. baking soda
- 2tbsp. lemon zest
- ¼tsp. salt
- ¾ cup canola oil
- 2tsp. vanilla
- ½ cup lemon juice

METHOD

1. Preheat your oven to 350°Fm and grease a cookie sheet.
2. Combine the flour, soda, sugar, salt, and zest.
3. Add the wet ingredients, and blend together well.
4. Drop teaspoonfuls about two inches apart onto your cookie sheet.
5. Bake for around ten minutes.

Oatmeal, Chocolate, and Peanut Butter Cookies

TIME: 20mins   **SERVES:** 36

INGREDIENTS

- ⅔ cup crunchy peanut butter
- 4tbsp. vegetable oil
- 2tbsp. crunchy peanut butter
- 2 cups light brown sugar
- 2tsp. pure vanilla extract
- ⅔ cup soymilk
- 1 cup whole wheat flour
- 1tsp. baking soda
- 1 cup all-purpose flour
- 1tsp. salt
- 1⅓ cups semi-sweet chocolate chips
- 2 cups rolled oats

METHOD

1. Preheat your oven to 375°F, and line a cookie sheet.
2. Combine all the ingredients until well blended.
3. Drop tablespoonfuls onto your baking sheet, and bake for ten minutes.

Scrumptious Soft Sugar Cookies

TIME: 30mins   **SERVES:** 12

INGREDIENTS

- ½ cup vegan margarine
- ½ cup sugar
- 1tsp. vanilla
- 3tbsp. extra-firm silken tofu, pureed
- 1¼ cups flour
- ¼tsp. salt
- 1tsp. baking powder

METHOD

1. Preheat your oven to 350°F.
2. Cream the margarine with the sugar until pale and fluffy.
3. Stir in the mashed tofu and vanilla.
4. Sift in the flour, baking powder, and salt, and mix well.
5. Roll into balls, then flatten onto an ungreased cookie sheet.
6. Bake for ten minutes.

Simple Chocolate Chip Cookies

TIME: 30mins   **SERVES:** 36

INGREDIENTS

- 1¼ cups sugar
- 1 cup margarine, softened
- 1tbsp. molasses
- 2½ cups all-purpose flour
- 2tsp. vanilla extract
- 1tsp. baking soda
- 1½ cups semi-sweet chocolate chips
- 1tsp. salt

METHOD

1. Preheat your oven to 350°F.
2. Cream the margarine with the sugar until pale and fluffy.
3. Stir in the molasses and vanilla until blended.
4. Sift in the dry ingredients, and mix to form a dough. Fold in the chocolate chips.
5. Roll into balls, and flatted onto a cookie sheet.
6. Bake for around eight to ten minutes.

Walnut and Chocolate Chip Cookies

Time: 20mins   **Serves:** 20-30

INGREDIENTS

- ½ cup brown sugar
- 1tsp. vanilla
- ½ cup white sugar
- ¼tsp. salt
- ½ cup margarine
- 1⅛ cups flour
- 1 egg substitute
- ½tsp. baking soda
- ½ cup walnuts
- 8oz. chocolate chips

METHOD

1. Preheat your oven to 375°F, and grease a cookie sheet.
2. Melt margarine in saucepan, then stir in the sugars.
3. Sift in the flour, baking soda, and salt, then add the egg replacer and vanilla.
4. Fold in the chocolate and nuts, then leave the dough in the fridge for an hour.
5. Bake for ten minutes.

Brownie-Oat Cookies

Time: 15mins   **Serves:** 20-30

INGREDIENTS

- ⅓ cup sugar
- ⅔ cup flour
- 1 cup oats
- 1tsp. baking powder
- ½ cup cocoa powder
- 1 egg substitute
- 1tsp. vanilla
- ⅓ cup maple syrup

METHOD

1. Preheat your oven to 350°F, and grease a cookie sheet.
2. Combine the egg replacer, vanilla, and syrup, then sift in the dry ingredients and incorporate.
3. Form into small balls, flatten, and bake for ten minutes.

Perfect Pumpkin Cookies

Time: 12mins

INGREDIENTS

- ½ cup olive oil
- 15oz. can pumpkin
- 1 cup sugar
- 1tsp. vanilla extract
- ½tsp. salt
- 2 cups all-purpose flour
- 1tbsp. baking powder
- 1 pinch coriander
- 1 pinch cardamom

METHOD

1. Preheat your oven to 375°F.
2. Combine the wet ingredients, then sift in the dry ingredients and blend together.
3. Bake for around ten minutes.

Chewy Peanut Butter Cookies

Time: 45mins   **Serves:** 24

INGREDIENTS

- ⅓ cup almond butter
- ⅓ cup peanut butter
- ⅓ cup margarine
- 1½tsp. Ener-G Egg

Substitute
- ⅔ cup brown sugar
- 2tbsp. water
- 1tsp. vanilla extract

- 2tbsp. soymilk
- ¾ cup all-purpose flour
- ⅛tsp. salt
- ½tsp. baking powder

METHOD

1. Preheat your oven to 375°F, and grease a cookie sheet.
2. Mix the water with the egg replacer, and set aside.
3. Cream the peanut butter with the almond butter, sugar and margarine.
4. Mix in the soymilk, egg replacer, and vanilla.
5. Sift in the flour, salt, and baking powder.
6. Place 2-inches apart on your cookie sheet, then bake for eight to fifteen minutes.

Chocolate Cookies

Time: 38mins

INGREDIENTS

- ¼ cup applesauce
- ¾ cup sugar
- 2tbsp. oil
- 3-4tbsp. water
- ½tsp. baking soda
- ¼tsp. salt
- 1 cup flour
- ¾ cup dairy-free semi-sweet chocolate chips
- ⅓ cup cocoa

METHOD

1. Cream together the oil, applesauce, sugar, and a tablespoon of water.
2. Add the rest of the water, and mix well.
3. Sift in all the dry ingredients, and blend together.
4. Fold in the chocolate chips.
5. Refrigerate for around an hour.
6. Preheat your oven 400°F, and grease a cookie sheet.
7. Roll into 24 balls, then bake for around eight minutes. They will harden as they cool.

Chocolate Chip and Cinnamon Cookies

Time: 20mins

INGREDIENTS

- 1¾ cups flour
- 2⅓ cups oats
- ⅔ cup white sugar
- 1tsp. cinnamon
- ½ cup vegan margarine
- 1tsp. baking soda
- 2 bananas, mashed
- ⅔ cup chocolate chips

METHOD

1. Preheat your oven to 350°F, and grease a baking sheet.
2. Combine the sugar, banana, and margarine.
3. Stir in oats, then add the rest of the dry ingredients.
4. Fold in the chocolate chips.
5. Spoon onto your baking sheet, and bake for ten minutes.

Super Sugar Cookies

Time: 35mins   **Serves:** 10

INGREDIENTS

- ¾ cup white sugar, preferably vegan
- 2 cups whole wheat pastry flour
- ½ cup white flour, for dusting
- ¼ cup applesauce
- 1tsp. baking powder
- ½ cup canola oil
- ½tsp. cinnamon
- 3-4tsp. vanilla extract

METHOD

1. Preheat your oven to 325°F, and grease a baking sheet.
2. Combine the pastry flour, baking powder, sugar, and cinnamon.
3. Whisk together the applesauce, oil and vanilla together until well combined.
4. Blend the two mixtures together, then knead into a dough.
5. Roll out to around a quarter-inch thick, then cut into cookies.
6. Bake for around ten minutes.

Cranberry and Oatmeal Cookies

Time: 16mins

INGREDIENTS

- ¼ cup peanut butter
- ½ cup sugar
- 2tbsp. vegan butter
- ¼ cup rice milk
- 1 cup whole wheat flour
- 1tsp. pure vanilla extract
- ½tsp. baking soda
- 1tsp. cinnamon
- ½tsp. salt
- ½tsp. nutmeg
- ¾ cup dried cranberries
- ¾ cup rolled oats

METHOD

1. Preheat your oven to 375°.
2. Mix together all the ingredients, then fold in the oats and cranberries.
3. Drop teaspoonfuls onto a greased baking sheet, then flatten.
4. Bake for around eight minutes.

Wheat-free Chocolate Chip Cookies

Time: 25mins   **Serves:** 9

INGREDIENTS

- ½tsp. baking soda
- ¼ cup brown sugar
- ¼tsp. salt
- ½ cup sugar
- 1tbsp flaxseed meal
- 1¾ cups oat flour
- ⅓ cup canola oil
- ¼ cup soymilk
- ¾ cup chocolate chips
- 1tsp. vanilla

METHOD

1. Preheat your oven to 375°F. Combine the oat flour, soda, and salt.
2. Combine the flaxseed meal and soymilk.
3. Stir in the sugar, vanilla, and oil, then sift in all the dry ingredients.
4. Fold in the chocolate chips, then drop tablespoonsful into a baking sheet, leaving plenty of space around each.   Bake for twelve to fifteen minutes.

Gingerbread Cookies

Time: 28mins

INGREDIENTS

- 1½ cups flour
- ½tsp. baking soda
- 1tsp. baking powder
- 1tsp. ground cinnamon
- ¼tsp. allspice
- ½tsp. ground ginger
- ¼tsp. salt
- ¼ cup sugar
- ⅓ cup vegetable shortening
- ⅓ cup molasses
- ½tsp. pure vanilla extract
- 2¼tbsp. hot water

METHOD

1. Combine all the dry ingredients.
2. Cream the shortening with the sugar, then stir in the molasses, hot water, and vanilla. Blend with the dry ingredients.
3. Refrigerate for two to four hours.   Preheat your oven to 400°F.
4. Roll out the dough, cut into shapes, then bake for eight to ten minutes.

Cowboy Cookies

Time: 31mins

INGREDIENTS

- 2 cups flour
- 2 cups quick-cooking oats
- 1tsp. baking soda
- ¼tsp. salt
- ½tsp. baking powder
- ⅔ cup oil
- ¾ cup brown sugar
- ⅔ cup sugar
- ½ cup non-dairy milk
- 1tsp. vanilla extract
- 1tbsp. ground flaxseeds
- 1 cup coconut, shredded
- unsweetened
- 1 cup pecan pieces, chopped and toasted
- 1 cup semisweet chocolate chips

METHOD

1. Preheat your oven to 350°F, and line a cookie sheet.
2. Mixed together the oats, baking soda, flour, baking powder, and salt.
3. Whisk together the oil, brown sugar, sugar, milk, flaxseeds, and vanilla.
4. Blend together the two mixtures, then fold in the coconut, chocolate chips, and pecans.
5. Drop large tablespoons onto a cookie sheet, leaving plenty of space between each.
6. Flatten, then bake for around fifteen minutes.

Mega Molasses Cookies

Time: 20mins   **Serves:** 14

INGREDIENTS

- 2tbsp. flour
- 1 cup flour
- 1tsp. baking soda
- ½tsp. ginger
- ½tsp. cinnamon
- ¼tsp. clove
- ½ cup packed brown sugar
- ⅛tsp. salt
- 6tbsp. vegetable oil
- ½tsp. vanilla extract
- 2tbsp. molasses
- 2tbsp. unsweetened applesauce
- 1tbsp. coarse sugar
- 3tbsp. sugar, for rolling

METHOD

1. Preheat your oven to 325°F.
2. Combine the flour, cinnamon, baking soda, ginger, cloves, and salt.
3. Combine the brown sugar, molasses, vegetable oil, vanilla, and apple sauce.
4. Combine the two mixtures until well blended.
5. Put dollops of the dough onto your cookie sheet, flatten, and sprinkle with sugar.
6. Bake for around thirteen to sixteen minutes.
7. Cool slightly, then transfer to a wire rack.

Oatmeal Raisin Cookies

Time: 35mins   **Serves:** 15-30

INGREDIENTS

- ½ cup applesauce
- 1½ bananas, mashed
- 2tsp. vanilla
- 1 cup flour
- ½ cup brown sugar
- 1½tsp. baking powder
- 1tsp. cinnamon
- 1 pinch salt
- 1 pinch nutmeg
- ¾ cup oatmeal
- 1 cup raisins

METHOD

1. Preheat your oven to 350°F, and line a cookie sheet.
2. Combine all the ingredients until well blended, then drop onto the cookie sheet.
3. Bake for twenty to thirty minutes.

Gluten-Free, Sugar-Free Chocolate Oatmeal Cookies

Time: 35mins**Serves:** 10

INGREDIENTS

- ½ cup agave nectar
- 5tbsp. coconut oil
- ¼ cup peach butter
- 1tsp. molasses
- 2tsp. gluten-free vanilla extract
- 3tbsp. water
- ¼tsp. almond extract
- 1½tsp. egg substitute, powder
- 1 cup gluten-free flour
- ½tsp. salt
- ½tsp. cinnamon
- ½tsp. baking soda
- 2 pinches nutmeg
- ½ cup chocolate chips
- 1½ cups gluten-free oats

METHOD

1. Preheat your oven to 350°F, and grease a cookie sheet.
2. Using a mixer, combine the coconut oil, agave nectar, apple butter, molasses, almond extract, vanilla, and water.
3. Sift in the dry ingredients, and blend well.
4. Drop teaspoonfuls onto the cookie sheet, and bake for twelve to fifteen minutes.

Quick Sugar Cookies

Time: 30mins

INGREDIENTS

- ½ cup cooking oil
- 1tsp. baking powder
- ¾ cup sugar
- ½ cup soymilk
- 2½ cups all-purpose flour
- 1tsp. almond extract

METHOD

1. Preheat your oven to 350°F, and line a cookie sheet.
2. Whisk together the oil, sugar, baking powder, soymilk, and almond extract.
3. Sift in the flour and combine.
4. Knead gently, then shape into balls and flatten onto the cookie sheet.
5. Bake for eight minutes.

Oatmeal and Apple Cookies

Time: 20mins **Serves:** 15-16

INGREDIENTS

- ½ cup white sugar
- ½ cup light brown sugar
- ¾ cup sweetened applesauce
- 1tsp. baking powder
- 1 cup whole wheat flour
- 1 pinch salt
- cinnamon, to sprinkle on top
- 1 cup rolled oats

METHOD

1. Preheat your oven to 375°F, and grease a cookie sheet.
2. Blend the sugars with the applesauce, then add the flour, baking powder, and salt.
3. Fold in the rolled oats.
4. Divide into cookies on your cookie sheet, and sprinkle with cinnamon.
5. Bake for ten minutes.

Chocolate Carob Farina Nut Cookies

Time: 25mins   **Serves:** 36

INGREDIENTS

- ⅓ cup peanut butter
- 1 cup sugar
- 2tbsp. canola oil
- ⅓ cup soymilk
- 1 cup whole wheat flour
- 1tsp. pure vanilla extract
- ½tsp. baking soda
- 1 cup farina
- ½tsp. salt
- ¼ cup chocolate chips
- ½ cup walnuts, chopped
- ¼ cup carob chips

METHOD

1. Preheat your oven to 425°F, and grease a baking sheet.
2. Thoroughly combine all the ingredients.
3. Roll into small balls, then flatten on the baking sheet.
4. Bake for five minutes, or until golden brown.
5. Cool for ten minutes before transferring to a wire rack.

No-Bake Oatmeal Chocolate Cookies

Time: 10mins **Serves:** 20-30

INGREDIENTS

- ½ cup soymilk
- ½ cup margarine
- 2 cups sugar
- 2½ cups oats
- ½ cup cocoa powder

METHOD

1. Put everything but the oats into a saucepan and boil for five minutes.
2. Remove from the heat and stir in the oats.
3. Shape into balls, cool on wax paper, and leave to cool.

Simple Sugar Cookies

Time: 16mins

INGREDIENTS

- ½ cup vegan butter
- 3tsp. Ener-G Egg Substitute
- ¾ cup sugar
- 4tbsp. water
- 2¼ cups flour
- ¼tsp. vanilla
- 1tsp. baking powder
- 2tbsp. rice milk
- ½tsp. salt

METHOD

1. Combine all the ingredients to form a dough, then refrigerate for at least two hours.
2. Preheat your oven to 350°F, and line a cookie sheet.
3. Roll your dough to around a quarter-inch thick, then cut into shapes.
4. Bake for around eight minutes, then cool before transferring to a wire rack.

Oaty Apple and Walnut Cookies

Time: 22mins

INGREDIENTS

- 2 cups old fashioned oats
- 1½ cups whole wheat flour
- ½ cup Splenda brown sugar blend
- ¼tsp. baking soda
- 1½tsp. baking powder
- ¼tsp. salt
- 4tsp. flaxseed meal
- 1¼tsp. cinnamon
- 5oz. dried apple rings, finely chopped
- 2tbsp. vegetable oil
- ½ cup walnuts, chopped
- 1 cup unsweetened applesauce
- ⅓-½ cup unsweetened apple juice
- 2tsp. vanilla

METHOD

1. Preheat your oven to 350°F.
2. Combine the flour, brown sugar, oats, baking powder, salt, baking soda, cinnamon, and flaxseed meal.
3. Stir in the chopped dried apple and walnuts.
4. Combine the applesauce, oil, vanilla, and 1/3-cup apple juice.
5. Gently blend the two mixtures.
6. Dollop onto your cookie sheet, then bake for twelve to fifteen minutes.

Peanut Butter and Oatmeal Cookies

Time: 25mins

INGREDIENTS

- 1 cup whole wheat flour
- 1½tsp. baking powder
- ⅓ cup all-purpose flour
- ¼tsp. baking soda
- 1¼tsp. cinnamon, ground
- ¼tsp. salt
- 2 cups oats
- ½ cup applesauce
- 1 cup dry roasted salted peanuts
- ½ cup creamy peanut butter
- ⅛ cup dark brown sugar
- ⅛ cup Splenda sugar substitute
- ⅓ cup non-dairy milk
- 1½tsp. pure vanilla extract
- 4tsp. ground flaxseeds

METHOD

1. Preheat your oven to 350°F, and line a cookie sheet.
2. Sift together the flours, baking soda, baking powder, cinnamon, salt, and oats. Stir in the peanuts.
3. Whisk together the applesauce, sugars, peanut butter, ground flaxseeds, and vanilla.
4. Blend the two mixtures, then dollop onto the cookie sheet and flatten.
5. Bake for fifteen minutes.

Macadamia and White Chocolate Cookies

Time: 22mins   **Serves:** 40

INGREDIENTS

- 1 cup brown sugar
- ½ cup Earth Balance vegan margarine, softened
- ½ cup sugar
- ½ cup vegetable shortening
- 1 egg substitute
- 1tsp. vanilla extract
- 2tbsp. applesauce
- 1tsp. baking soda
- 2¼ cups all-purpose flour
- ¼tsp. salt
- ½ cup macadamia nuts, chopped
- ¾ cup white chocolate, chopped

METHOD

1. Preheat your oven to 350°F.
2. Beat together the sugars, shortening, butter, egg replacer, vanilla, and applesauce.
3. Sift in the dry ingredients, and blend together.
4. Fold in the nuts and chocolate.
5. Drop two-inches apart onto a cookie sheet.
6. Bake for ten to twelve minutes.

Cranberry and Pumpkin Cookies

Time: 15mins   **Serves:** 14

INGREDIENTS

- 1 cup stevia
- 2 cups whole wheat flour
- 1½ cups rolled oats
- 1½tsp. baking soda
- ½tsp. salt
- ½tsp. baking powder
- ½tsp. cinnamon
- ¼tsp. clove
- ½tsp. ginger
- ¼tsp. allspice
- ½ cup water
- 1 cup pumpkin
- 2tbsp. egg substitute
- 1 cup cranberries, quartered
- 1tsp. vanilla extract

METHOD

1. Preheat your oven to 350°F. Combine all the ingredients until well blended.
2. Dollop onto a cookie sheet, then flatten.   Bake for fifteen minutes.

Butter Almond Cookies

Time: 19mins**Serves:** 12

INGREDIENTS

- 1 cup flour
- ½tsp. baking soda
- 1tsp. baking powder
- 2tbsp. brown sugar
- ⅓ cup almond butter
- ½tsp. salt
- ½ cup maple syrup
- 3tbsp. canola oil
- ½tsp. vanilla extract

METHOD

1. Preheat your oven to 350°F.
2. Combine all the ingredients together, then roll into balls and flatten onto a cookie sheet, well-spaced.
3. Bake for around nine minutes.

Carob Spelt Cookies

Time: 35mins

INGREDIENTS

- ¾ cup sugar
- ½ cup vegan margarine
- 1 banana
- ½tsp. baking powder
- 1tsp. vanilla extract
- 1¼ cups light spelt flour
- ½ cup carob chips
- ½tsp. salt

METHOD

1. Preheat your oven to 350°F, and line a cookie sheet.
2. Beat the margarine with the vanilla, sugar, and banana.
3. Add the flour, baking powder, and salt, and blend gently.
4. Fold in the carob chips.
5. Dollop onto your cookie sheet, then bake for ten to fourteen minutes.

Brownie-Style Oat Cookies

Time: 16mins

INGREDIENTS

- ⅔ cup flour
- ¼ cup sugar
- ¾ cup oats
- ¼tsp. salt
- ¼ cup carob powder
- 1½tsp. Ener-G Egg Substitute
- 1tsp. baking powder
- 2tbsp. water
- ¼ cup maple syrup
- 1tsp. vanilla

METHOD

1. Preheat your oven to 350°F.
2. Combine all your ingredients until well mixed.
3. Bake for around eight minutes.

Chocolate and Hazelnut Cookies

Time: 35mins   **Serves:** 18

INGREDIENTS

- ½ cup hazelnuts
- ½ cup whole wheat flour
- ½ cup white flour
- ¾ cup white sugar
- ⅛tsp. salt
- 1tsp. baking powder
- ¼ cup unsweetened cocoa powder
- ½tsp. vanilla extract
- ¼ cup vegan margarine
- ¼ cup soymilk, plus 1tbsp. soymilk
- 4½tbsp. warm water
- 1½tbsp. ground flaxseeds

METHOD

1. Preheat your oven to 325°F.
2. Combine the ground flaxseeds with the water and leave to thicken.
3. Combine all the ingredients until well incorporated.
4. Dollop onto a greased cookie sheet, well-spaced.
5. Cook for around ten to fifteen minutes.

Sugar-free Oatmeal and Cranberry Cookies

Time: 17mins   **Serves:** 16

INGREDIENTS

- 1 cup traditional oatmeal
- ½tsp. cinnamon
- ½tsp. baking powder
- 1 pinch salt
- 2tbsp. real maple syrup
- ¼ cup dried cranberries
- 1 cup whole wheat pastry flour
- ¼ cup agave syrup
- 1½tsp. vanilla
- ¼ cup canola oil

METHOD

1. Preheat your oven to 375°F.
2. Mix everything together well.
3. Dollop onto a lined cookie sheet, then bake for ten minutes.

Scrumptious Sugar Cookies

Time: 20mins

INGREDIENTS

- ¾ cup sugar
- ¼ cup applesauce
- 1tsp. baking powder
- 2 cups flour, sifted
- ½ cup oil
- 1 pinch cinnamon
- 1tbsp. vanilla extract
- candy sprinkles, to decorate
- sugar, to decorate

METHOD

1. Preheat your oven to 350°F, and line a cookie sheet.
2. Combine all the ingredients to form a dough.
3. Roll out and cut into cookies.
4. Bake for ten to twelve minutes.

Chewy Peanut Butter Cookies

Time: 13mins   **Serves:** 18

INGREDIENTS

- 3⁄4 cup smooth peanut butter
- 11⁄4 cups firmly packed light brown sugar
- 1⁄2 cup applesauce
- 1tbsp. soymilk
- 1tbsp. vanilla extract
- 13⁄4 cups unbleached all-purpose flour
- 3⁄4tsp. salt
- 3⁄4tsp. baking soda

METHOD

1. Preheat your oven to 375°F, and line a cookie sheet.
2. Cream together the brown sugar with the peanut butter.
3. Mix in the applesauce, soymilk, and vanilla extract.
4. Stir in the baking soda, salt, and flour.
5. Dollop onto your cookie sheet, and flatten with the prongs of a fork.
6. Bake for eight to ten minutes, then leave to cool slightly before transferring to a wire rack.

Cornmeal and Thyme Cookies

Time: 32mins   **Serves:** 6

INGREDIENTS

- 13⁄4 cups white spelt flour
- 1 cup cornmeal
- 1tsp. baking soda
- 1⁄2tsp. salt
- 11⁄4 cups raw sugar
- 8oz. vegan margarine, softened
- 2tsp. egg substitute mixed with 4tbsp. filtered water
- 11⁄4tbsp. thyme, finely chopped
- 3⁄4 cup dried currants

METHOD

1. Preheat your oven to 350°F, and line your baking sheets.
2. Combine the flour, cornmeal, baking soda, and salt.
3. Cream together the margarine and sugar, then mix in the egg replacer.
4. Stir in the flour mix until just combined, then fold in the currants and thyme.
5. Dollop, well-spaced, onto a cookie sheet.   Bake for around ten to twelve minutes.

Simple Healthy Cookies

Time: 29mins**Serves:** 10-12

INGREDIENTS

- 1⁄2 cup barley flour, 1tbsp. barley flour
- 1⁄2tsp. baking powder
- 1⁄4 cup spelt flour
- 1⁄2 cup sunflower seeds
- 1⁄4 cup pumpkin seeds
- 1⁄4 cup hemp seeds
- 1⁄4 cup raisins
- 1tsp. salt
- 3-4tbsp. non-dairy chocolate chips
- 2tbsp. flaxseed meal
- 2tbsp. chocolate soymilk
- 1⁄4 cup pure maple syrup
- 11⁄2tsp. blackstrap molasses
- 3tbsp. canola oil
- 1tsp. vanilla extract

METHOD

1. Preheat your oven to 350°F, and grease a cookie sheet.
2. Mix the flaxseed, maple syrup, and milk, then add the rest of the wet ingredients.
3. Combine the dry ingredients, and mix with the wet ingredients.
4. Shape into balls, and add to the cookie sheet.   Bake for thirteen to fourteen minutes.

Perfect Peanut Butter Cookies

Time: 20mins

INGREDIENTS

- 3⁄4 cup old fashioned oats
- 1⁄4tgsp. salt
- 1tsp. baking powder
- 1 cup all-purpose flour
- 1 cup creamy peanut butter
- 1⁄2 cup sugar
- 1⁄8 cup soymilk

METHOD

1. Preheat your oven to 375°F, and grease a cookie sheet.
2. Combine your flour, salt, and baking powder.
3. Melt the peanut butter in your microwave, then add the soymilk and sugar.
4. Add to the flour mix, and combine.   Fold in the oats.
5. Dollop onto the cookie sheet, and flatten with a fork.   Bake for around ten minutes.

Chocolate Whoopi Pies

Time: 1hr

INGREDIENTS

COOKIES

- 3⁄4 cup vegetable shortening
- 2tsp. vanilla extract
- 1 cup sugar
- 1⁄2 cup soymilk
- 3⁄4 cup cocoa powder
- 11⁄2 cups all-purpose flour
- 2tsp. cornstarch
- 1⁄4tsp. baking soda
- 1⁄2tsp. salt

FILLING

- 1⁄4 cup vegetable shortening
- 1tsp. pure vanilla extract
- 1⁄4 cup margarine, softened
- 23⁄4 cups powdered sugar

METHOD

1. Preheat your oven to 325°F, and line a cookie sheet.
2. Make the cookies by creaming the shortening with the sugar.
3. Add the vanilla and milk, then the rest of the ingredients.
4. Roll into balls and flatten onto your cookie sheet.   Bake for around twelve minutes.
5. To make the filling, cream the margarine and shortening, then slowly add the sugar.
6. Sandwich between two cookies.

Pumpkin and Chocolate Cookies

Time: 27mins   Serves: 15

INGREDIENTS

- 6tbsp. sugar
- 1tbsp. corn oil
- 11tbsp. pumpkin puree
- 1⁄2tbsp. flaxseed meal
- 1⁄2tsp. vanilla extract
- 11⁄2tbsp. water
- 1 cup flour
- 1⁄2tsp. baking soda
- 1tsp. baking powder
- 1⁄2tsp. cinnamon
- 1⁄4 cup semisweet vegan chocolate chips
- 1⁄4tsp. salt

METHOD

1. Preheat your oven to 375°F. Boil the water, then add to flaxseed meal, and leave to thicken.
2. Combine the sugar, oil, pumpkin, vanilla, and flax meal mix.
3. Stir in the flour, baking soda, baking powder, cinnamon, and salt.
4. Fold in the chocolate chips, then bake for ten to twelve minutes.

Raisin and Oatmeal Cookies

Time: 25mins

INGREDIENTS

- 2 cups apple juice, boiling
- 1½ cups rolled oats, toasted
- ¼ cup brown rice flour
- ½ cup whole wheat pastry flour
- 2tbsp. sesame oil
- 1tsp. cinnamon
- ½ cup raisins
- 1tsp. vanilla

METHOD

1. Preheat your oven to 375°F, and line a cookie sheet.
2. Bring the apple juice to a boil, then remove from the heat. Stir in the oats, and leave to rest for five minutes.
3. Combine with the rest of the ingredients, then dollop onto the baking sheet.
4. Bake for fifteen minutes.

Almond and Jam Cookies

Time: 25mins   **Serves:** 7

INGREDIENTS

- 1½ cups brown rice flour
- ¼ cup almonds
- 1 pinch salt
- ¼ cup maple syrup
- ⅛-¼tsp. cinnamon
- ⅛ cup oil
- 2tbsp. jam
- ⅛ cup applesauce

METHOD

1. Preheat your oven to 350°F.
2. Combine all the ingredients bar the jam together, then roll into balls and flatten into cookies.
3. Dollop a bit of jam onto each cookie.
4. Bake for fifteen to twenty minutes.

Gluten-Free Gingerbread Cookies

Time: 8hrs   **Serves:** 20

INGREDIENTS

- 100g. buckwheat flour
- 3tbsp. carob powder
- 100g. rolled oats, ground into flour
- 1tsp. cinnamon
- ¼tsp. ground cloves
- 1tsp. ground ginger
- ¼tsp. ground nutmeg
- ¼tsp. ground allspice
- ¼tsp. cardamom
- 3 pinches black pepper
- ¼ cup applesauce
- 100g. almonds, ground into meal
- ½tbsp. ground chia seeds
- 10 drops liquid stevia
- ½ cup oat milk
- 3tbsp. artificial sweetener
- ¼tsp. salt
- 1tbsp. peanut butter
- 1tbsp. almond butter

METHOD

1. Combine the dry ingredients.
2. Whisk together the wet ingredients.
3. Mix together until a dough forms, then cover and refrigerate overnight.
4. Preheat your oven to 350°F, and line a baking sheet.
5. Roll out your dough on a floured surface, and cut into cookies.
6. Bake for around fourteen minutes.

Oatmeal Snickerdoodles

Time: 30mins   **Serves:** 8

INGREDIENTS

- 1½ cups oats
- 5tbsp. water
- 5tbsp. sugar
- 1tsp. baking powder
- 2tbsp. applesauce
- ¼ cup sugar
- 2tsp. cinnamon

METHOD

1. Preheat your oven to 350°F. Combine all but the last two ingredients, until well blended.
2. Mix the sugar and cinnamon, the scatter on a flat surface.
3. Roll the dough into balls, then roll these in the sugar mix.
4. Flatten onto a cookie sheet, then bake for ten minutes.

Nutella-Stuffed Oatmeal and Peanut Butter Cookies

Time: 34mins   **Serves:** 10

INGREDIENTS

- ¾tsp. baking soda
- ½ cup peanut butter
- 2 cups oats
- 1⅓ cups flour
- ½ cup coconut oil
- 1 cup sugar
- ½ cup Nutella
- ¾ cup hemp milk

METHOD

1. Preheat your oven to 350°F.
2. Combine the flour and baking powder, then stir in the oats.
3. Combine the coconut oil, sugar, hemp milk, and peanut butter, then combine with the flour mixture.
4. Dollop onto a cookie sheet, and flatten.
5. Spread a little Nutella on each, then top with the remaining dough.   Bake for around fourteen minutes.

Cherry Bon-Bons

Time: 1hr 20mins   **Serves:** 24

INGREDIENTS

COOKIES

- ¾ cup powdered sugar
- 1tsp. vanilla extract
- 2tbsp. original soymilk
- 1½ cups unbleached all-purpose flour
- ½ cup vegan margarine
- 24 maraschino cherries
- ⅛tsp. salt

ICING

- 1 cup powdered sugar
- 2tbsp. maraschino cherry juice
- 1tbsp. vegan margarine

METHOD

1. Preheat your oven to 350°F.
2. Cream the Earth Balance with the powdered sugar until light and fluffy, then add the soymilk and vanilla extract.
3. Combine the flour and salt, then slowly add this to the creamed mixture.
4. Form into a dough, then divide into 24 portions.
5. Shape each bit around a cherry, and smooth around.
6. Bake for eighteen to twenty minutes.
7. To make the glaze, combine the powdered sugar, melted Earth Balance, and cherry juice, the drizzle this over your bon bons.

Chocolate and Raisin Cookies

Time: 1hr 25mins

INGREDIENTS

- 8oz. vegan butter
- 1tsp. baking soda
- 1tsp. salt
- 1¼ cups granulated sugar
- 1½tsp. canola oil
- 2½ cups unbleached all-purpose flour
- 1tbsp. packed brown sugar
- 2tsp. vanilla extract
- ½ cup raisins
- 1 cup semisweet vegan chocolate chips

METHOD

1. Preheat your oven to 350°F.
2. Sift together the flour, baking soda, and salt.
3. Cream together the margarine and sugar until light and fluffy.
4. Add the brown sugar, canola oil, and vanilla.
5. Stir in the flour mix, then fold in the chocolate chips and raisins.
6. Shape into balls, then flatten on a cookie sheet.
7. Bake for fifteen to seventeen minutes.

Cinnamon and Walnut Cookies

Time: 20mins   **Serves:** 8-10

INGREDIENTS

- 1 cup walnut halves
- 1tsp. grapeseed oil
- 5 dates, pitted and roughly chopped
- 1½tsp. vanilla extract
- 1 pinch salt
- 1tsp. ground cinnamon

METHOD

1. Preheat your oven to 350°F.
2. Blitz the walnuts and dates in a food processor, pulse until coarsely ground.
3. Add the oil, cinnamon, vanilla, and salt.
4. Dollop onto a lined cookie sheet, then flatten.
5. Bake for six to eight minutes.

Simple Peanut Butter Cookies

Time: 20mins   **Serves:** 30

INGREDIENTS

- ½ cup sugar
- ½ cup peanut butter
- ½ cup brown sugar
- ¼ cup shortening
- ⅛ cup applesauce
- ¼ cup vegan butter
- 1tbsp. egg substitute powder
- 1¼ cups all-purpose flour
- 3tbsp. water
- ¾tsp. baking soda
- ¼tsp. salt
- ½tsp. baking powder

METHOD

1. Preheat your oven to 375°F.
2. Combine all your ingredients well.
3. Shape into balls and place on your cookie sheet. Flatten with a fork.
4. Bake for around ten minutes.

Banana and Persimmon Cookies and Dark Rum

Time: 27mins   **Serves:** 8

INGREDIENTS

- 2 ripe persimmons
- 1tsp. baking soda
- 2 ripe bananas
- ½ cup vegan butter
- 1½tsp. egg substitute

- ¾ cup sugar
- 2tbsp. warm water
- 1tsp. baking soda
- 2 cups flour
- ½tsp. cinnamon

- ½tsp. dried ginger
- ½tsp. clove
- ½tsp. salt
- 1tsp. vanilla extract
- 1 cup walnuts, chopped

METHOD

1. Preheat your oven to 350°F, and line a cookie sheet.
2. In a food processor, blend the persimmons and bananas with a teaspoon of vanilla extract. Blend until smooth. Add a teaspoon of baking soda and blend again. Cream the butter with the sugar.
3. Blend your egg replacer with two teaspoons of warm water, then stir into the creamed butter and sugar.
4. Stir in the dry ingredients and fruit puree, then fold in the walnuts.
5. Dollop onto the cookie sheet, leaving plenty of space between each. Bake for around twelve minutes.
6. Combine icing sugar with dark rum, then drizzle over the cooked cookies.

Kahlua and Double Chocolate Cookies

Time: 20mins   **Serves:** 36

INGREDIENTS

- ⅔ cup unsweetened cocoa powder
- ½tsp. salt
- 1tsp. baking soda
- ⅔ cup canola oil
- 4tsp. flaxseeds (ground)

- 1½ cups sugar
- ¼ cup soymilk
- 2tsp. pure vanilla extract
- 2 cups whole wheat pastry flour
- ¼ cup Kahlua

- ½tsp. almond extract
- ¾ cup walnuts, toasted and chopped
- ¾ cup semisweet vegan chocolate chips

METHOD

1. Preheat your oven to 350°F.   Combine the sugar, oil, flaxseeds, soymilk, almond extract, and vanilla.
2. Combine the flour, baking soda, cocoa, and salt.
3. Blend the two mixtures, then fold in the chocolate and walnuts.
4. Roll into balls, then flatten onto a lined cookie sheet.   Bake for around ten minutes.

Iced Pumpkin Cookies

Time: 40mins   **Serves:** 36

INGREDIENTS

- 2 cups flour
- 1tsp. baking powder
- 1tsp. baking soda
- 2tsp. cinnamon
  ICING
- 3tbsp. soymilk
- 2 cups confectioners' sugar

- ½tsp. salt
- ½tsp. nutmeg
- ½ cup vegan margarine
- ½ cup agave nectar

- 1tsp. vanilla
- 1tbsp. melted vegan margarine

- 1 cup sugar
- 1 cup pumpkin puree
- 1tsp. vanilla
- egg replacement for 1 egg

METHOD

1. Preheat the oven to 350°F.   Combine all your ingredients well.
2. Dollop onto a lined cooked sheet, leaving plenty of space between each cookie.
3. Bake for around twenty minutes, then leave to cool for ten minutes before moving to a cooling rack.
4. For the icing, combine all the ingredients, then spoon over the completely cooled cookies.

Banana Breakfast Cookies

Time: 30mins   **Serves:** 24

INGREDIENTS

- ½ cup unsweetened applesauce
- 2 ripe bananas
- ½ cup maple syrup
- 2 cups rolled oats
- 2tsp. vanilla extract
- 1 cup white whole wheat flour
- 2tsp. cinnamon
- 2tsp. baking soda
- 1tsp. ground ginger
- 1 large navel orange, zest of
- ½tsp. nutmeg
- ½ cup walnuts, chopped
- ½ cup dried apricot, chopped
- ½ cup dried cranberries

METHOD

1. Preheat your oven to 350°F.
2. Mash your bananas, then add the applesauce, maple syrup, and vanilla.
3. Sift together the dry ingredients, the combine with the wet.
4. Fold in the zest, walnuts, and fruit.
5. Dollop onto a lined cookie sheet, flatten slightly, and bake for fifteen minutes.

Oreo-Style Cookies

Time: 5hrs 25mins   **Serves:** 5

INGREDIENTS

COOKIE
- 1 cup ground nuts
- 4 dates, pitted
  FILLING
- 1tsp. vanilla
- ⅔ cup coconut butter
- ¼ cup shredded coconut
- 1tsp. vanilla extract
- ½tsp. lemon juice
- 1tbsp. Agave
- ⅓ cup cacao, powder
- 2tbsp. Agave
- 2tbsp. tahini

METHOD

1. To make the cookies, chuck all the ingredients in your blend, and blend until it forms a dough.
2. Roll on a floured surface, and cut into cookies.
3. Dehydrate in your dehydrator for four to five hours, at 105°.
4. To make the filling, mix all the ingredients together. Spread on half the cookies, then sandwich with the other half.

The Best Choc Chip Cookies

Time: 32mins

INGREDIENTS

- 2 cups unbleached white flour
- ½tsp. salt
- 2tsp. baking soda
- 5tbsp. cocoa powder
- ¾ cup semi-sweet chocolate chips
- ½tsp. cinnamon
- ⅓ cup water
- ¼ cup brown rice syrup
- ¾ cup turbinado sugar
- 1tsp. vanilla extract
- ½ cup olive oil
- 1tbsp. cocoa powder

METHOD

1. Preheat your oven to 350°F.
2. Combine all your ingredients until well incorporated.
3. Shape into balls, then flatten onto a lined baking sheet.
4. Bake for twelve to fourteen minutes.

Cranberry and Currant Cookies

Time: 22mins   **Serves:** 15

INGREDIENTS

- 1¼ cups unbleached all-purpose flour
- ¾ cup light brown sugar
- ¾tsp. ground cinnamon
- 1tsp. baking powder
- 1¾ cups rolled oats
- ¼ cup soymilk
- ½ cup dried cranberries
- 1 pinch salt
- ½ cup dried currant
- ½ cup applesauce
- ½ cup margarine
- 1tsp. baking powder

METHOD

1. Preheat your oven to 350°F, and grease some baking sheets.
2. Combine your flour, cinnamon baking powder, and salt.
3. Cream together the margarine, soymilk, sugar, and egg replacement.
4. Combine the two mixtures, then stir in the currants, oats, and cranberries.
5. Dollop onto baking sheets, at least two-inches apart.
6. Bake for twelve to fifteen minutes.

Lemon and Poppyseed Cookies

Time: 18mins   **Serves:** 10-15

INGREDIENTS

- ¾ cup brown sugar
- ¾ cup soy yogurt
- ¾ cup margarine
- 1½tsp. vanilla
- ¾tsp. salt
- ¾tsp. baking soda
- ¾ cup sugar
- 1tsp. lemon zest
- ⅓ cup poppy seeds
- 2½ cups flour

METHOD

1. Preheat your oven to 350°F.
2. Cream your sugar with the brown sugar and margarine, then add the soy yogurt and vanilla.
3. Add everything else, and combine.
4. Dollop onto a cookie sheet, and bake for eight to nine minutes.

Spiced Gingerbread Cookies

Time: 27mins   **Serves:** 30

INGREDIENTS

- ¼ cup margarine, softened
- ½ cup brown sugar
- ¾ cup dark molasses
- 3½ cups whole wheat flour
- ⅓ cup cold water
- 2tsp. baking soda
- ½tsp. salt
- 2tsp. baking powder
- 1tsp. allspice
- 1tsp. cinnamon
- 1tsp. clove

METHOD

1. Combine all your ingredients, then pop in the fridge for a few hours.
2. Preheat your oven to 350°F.
3. Roll out to a quarter-inch thick, cut into cookies, and place on a lined tray.
4. Bake for ten to twelve minutes.

Oatmeal Carob Cookies

Time: 17mins

INGREDIENTS

- 1tsp. baking soda
- 1 cup whole grain wheat flour
- ⅓ cup brown sugar
- 1½tbsp. carob powder
- ⅓ cup rolled oats
- ½ cup vanilla-flavored soymilk
- 2tbsp. almonds, chopped
- ½tbsp. vanilla extract
- ⅓ cup vegetable oil
- 1 pinch salt
- 1 pinch cinnamon

METHOD

1. Preheat your oven to 350°F.
2. Combine all your ingredients, then shape into balls.
3. Flatten onto a greased cookie sheet, about two inches apart.
4. Bake for eight to twelve minutes.

Gluten-Free Oatmeal and Pumpkin Cookies

Time: 45mins   **Serves:** 24

INGREDIENTS

- 1 cup softened virgin coconut oil
- 1½ cups coconut sugar
- 1 cup pumpkin puree
- ¼ cup ground flaxseeds
- 3 cups oat flour
- 1tbsp. vanilla extract
- 1 cup rolled oats
- ¾tsp. salt
- ¾tsp. baking soda
- 3-4tsp. cinnamon
- ½tsp. ground nutmeg
- 1tsp. ground ginger

METHOD

1. Preheat your oven to 350°F.
2. Combine all your ingredients well, then leave to rest for twenty minutes.
3. Dollop onto a cookie sheet, then bake for twelve to fifteen minutes.

Banana and Prune Cookies

Time: 40mins   **Serves:** 15-20

INGREDIENTS

- 4 bananas, mashed
- ½tsp. salt
- 1tsp. vanilla
- 1 cup prunes, chopped
- ¼ cup flaxseed meal
- 1 cup raisins
- ½ cup unsweetened dried shredded coconut
- 1 cup rolled oats
- ½ cup nuts, chopped

METHOD

1. Preheat your oven to 350°F.
2. Combine all your ingredients well, leaving the oats until laste.
3. Dollop onto a cookie sheet, then flatten with a fork.
4. Bake for around twenty minutes.

Raspberry and Almond Thumbprint Cookies

Time: 25mins

INGREDIENTS

- 2 cups whole wheat pastry flour
- 2tsp. baking powder
- 1 cup ground almonds
- ¼tsp. salt
- ⅓ cup orange juice
- ⅓ cup safflower oil
- ⅓ cup maple syrup
- ¼tsp. vanilla
- 1½tsp. almond extract
- raspberry preserves, for filling

METHOD

5. Preheat you oven to 350°F.
6. Sift together all the dry ingredients.
7. Combine the oil, syrup, juice, and extract together.
8. Blend together the two mixtures.
9. Form into balls, then flatten onto a lined baking sheet.
10. Make an indent in each with your thumb, and dot with raspberry preserve.
11. Bake for fifteen minutes.

Iced Peanut Butter and Chocolate Cookies

Time: 23mins   **Serves:** 12

INGREDIENTS

- 1¼ cups whole wheat flour
- ½ cup sugar
- ½ cup vegan margarine
- ⅓ cup brown sugar
- 1tsp. water
- 2tsp. vanilla
- ½tsp. salt
- 2½tbsp. cocoa powder
- ½tsp. baking soda
- 1tbsp. cocoa powder
- ½tsp. cinnamon
- 3tbsp. peanut butter

METHOD

1. Preheat your oven to 350°F.
2. Sift together your dry ingredients.
3. Cream your margarine with your sugar, then add the vanilla and water.
4. Blend with your dry ingredients.
5. Dollop onto a lined baking sheet, and cook for eight to ten minutes.
6. Warm the peanut butter in the microwave, then stir in the cinnamon and cocoa powder.
7. Drizzle over the cooled cookies.

Wholesome Walnut and Chocolate Chip Cookies

Time: 38mins

INGREDIENTS

- 2½ cups spelt flour
- ¾ cup virgin coconut oil
- 1 cup rolled oats
- ¾ cup agave nectar
- 1¼ cups chocolate chips
- 1tsp. salt
- 1 cup walnuts
- 2tbsp. water
- 1tbsp. vanilla extract

METHOD

1. Preheat your oven to 350°F.
2. Combine all your ingredients well, then shape into cookies.
3. Bake for 18 to 24 minutes.

Chocolate Maple Cookies

Time: 22mins   **Serves:** 11

INGREDIENTS

- 1 cup white flour
- ½ cup cocoa powder
- 1 cup wheat flour
- 1tsp. baking soda
- ½tsp. salt
- 1tsp. baking powder
- 1 cup maple syrup
- ½ cup vegetable oil
- ⅓ cup blackberry jam
- 2tsp. vanilla
- 12oz. semi-sweet chocolate chips
- ½ cup chopped pecans
- cooking spray

METHOD

1. Preheat your oven to 350°F.
2. In your food processor, blitz the flour, chocolate powder, wheat flour, baking soda, salt, and baking powder. Reserve.
3. Blitz your maple syrup, oil, jam, and vanilla in your food processor, then return the flour mix, and blend until smooth.
4. Fold in the pecans and chocolate chips.
5. Dollop onto a sprayed cookie tray, and bake for around ten minutes.

Carrot and Pecan Breakfast Cookies

Time: 30mins

INGREDIENTS

- ¼ cup brown sugar
- ¼ cup soymilk
- ¼ cup agave nectar
- ¼ cup vegan margarine
- 1tbsp. vanilla
- 6oz. silken tofu
- 1 banana, mashed
- 1tsp. baking powder
- 2 cups whole wheat pastry flour
- ¼tsp. salt
- 1 cup oatmeal
- 1tsp. cinnamon
- 1 large apple
- 1 cup pecans, chopped
- 1 cup carrot, shredded

METHOD

1. Preheat your oven to 350°F.
2. Sift together all the dry ingredients, then cream together the wets. Combine the two mixtures.
3. Fold in the apple, carrot, and nuts.
4. Bake for fourteen minutes.

Spiced Cookies

Time: 35mins

INGREDIENTS

- ¾ cup margarine
- ⅓ cup sugar
- 1tsp. vanilla
- ¾ cup brown sugar
- ½ cup soymilk
- ½tsp. baking soda
- 1 cup flour
- ¼tsp. ginger powder
- ½tsp. cinnamon
- ¼tsp. clove
- ¼tsp. nutmeg
- 1 cup dried cranberries
- 3 cups rolled oatmeal

METHOD

1. Preheat your oven to 350°F.
2. Cream the margarine with the sugars, then add the vanilla and soymilk.
3. Stir in the flour, baking soda, and spices, then fold in the oats and cranberries.
4. Spoon onto an ungreased cookie sheet, and bake for ten to fifteen minutes.

Choco-Banana Cookies

Time: 40mins   **Serves:** 4

INGREDIENTS

- 1½ cups chocolate chips
- ¼ cup white sugar
- 1 cup brown sugar
- ¼ cup banana, mashed
- 2½tsp. baking soda
- 1¼tsp. vanilla
- 2tbsp. applesauce
- 1¼ cups flour
- 1tsp. olive oil

METHOD

1. Preheat your oven to 350°F.
2. Combine all the ingredients, then fold in the chocolate chips.
3. Bake on a greased cookie sheet for fifteen to twenty minutes.

Oatmeal and Cranberry Cookies

Time: 32mins   **Serves:** 36

INGREDIENTS

- ½tsp. baking soda
- ½tsp. salt
- 1tsp. cinnamon
- 1 egg substitute
- ½ cup applesauce
- 1 cup sugar
- 1tbsp. maple syrup
- 1½ cups whole wheat flour
- 1¾ cups rolled oats
- ¼ cup soymilk
- ½ cup raisins
- ¾ cup semi-sweet chocolate chips
- ½ cup dried cranberries

METHOD

1. Preheat your oven to 350°F.
2. Combine all your ingredients until well combined.
3. Dollop onto a greased baking sheet, and bake for ten to twelve minutes.
4. Leave to harden before removing from the baking sheet.

No-Bake Jammy Banana-Oatmeal Cookies

Time: 20mins   **Serves:** 5

INGREDIENTS

- 2 cups all-bran cereal, crushed
- ½ cup cranberries
- 1 cup granola cereal
- ½ cup raisins
- ¼ cup walnuts, chopped
- ½ cup almonds, chopped
- 1 banana, mashed
- 1tbsp. jam
- 2tbsp. peanut butter

METHOD

1. Combine the bran cereal, cranberries, granola, raisins, walnuts, almonds.
2. Stir in the banana and jam.
3. Melt the peanut butter in the microwave, then stir this into your cookie dough.
4. Shape into cookies, then wrap each cookie in cling-wrap. Freeze overnight.

Superfood Cookies

Time: 27mins

INGREDIENTS

- 3/4 cup sugar
- 1tsp. baking powder
- 1tsp. vanilla extract
- 1/2 cup dairy-free margarine
- 1/4 cup olive oil
- 3/4 cup cranberries
- 2 cups flour

METHOD

1. Preheat your oven to 190°C.
2. Cream the margarine, sugar, and vanilla until light and fluffy, then stir in the oil.
3. Sift the flour and baking powder together, then mix into the creamed mixture.
4. Fold in the cranberries.
5. Roll into balls, then flatten onto a cookie tray.   Bake for around twelve minutes.

Chia and Chocolate Oatmeal Cookies

Time: 22mins   **Serves:** 48

INGREDIENTS

- 1/2 cup buckwheat flour
- 1/3 cup cocoa powder
- 1/3 cup cornstarch
- 1/4tsp. baking powder
- 1/3 cup unsweetened applesauce
- 1/3 cup soymilk
- 1/4tsp. baking soda
- 1tsp. vanilla
- 1tsp. chia seeds, ground
- 1/2 cup erythritol
- 1 cup oats
- 1tbsp. coconut oil, melted
- 3/8 cup dark chocolate, chopped
- 1tbsp. water

METHOD

1. Preheat your oven to 350°F.
2. Grind your chia seeds, then combine with the milk, erythritol, applesauce, and vanilla.
3. Combine the oats, cornstarch, buckwheat flour, baking powder, and soda, then stir in the chopped chocolate.
4. Rub your melted coconut oil into the dry ingredients, then stir in the wet ingredients and combine.
5. Dollop onto a cookie sheet, flatten, and bake for ten to twelve minutes.

Pumpkin and Coconut Cookies

Time: 35mins   **Serves:** 6

INGREDIENTS

- 1/2 cup almond flour
- 1/2tsp. baking powder
- 2tbsp. rice flour
- 1/4tsp. baking soda
- 2tbsp. coconut sugar
- crystals
- 1/2 cup quick-cooking oats
- 2tbsp. artificial sweetener
- 1 pinch salt
- 4tbsp. virgin coconut oil
- 1tsp. pumpkin spice
- 3tbsp. pumpkin puree
- 1 pinch ground cloves
- 1/4 cup raisins

METHOD

1. Preheat your oven to 350°F, and line a baking sheet.
2. Sift together all the dry ingredients except the cloves.
3. Add the wet ingredients, and mix well.
4. Shape into cookies, then decorate the top with dried fruits and nuts, and sprinkle with ground cloves.
5. Bake for 25 minutes, then turn off the oven but let the cookies sit in the residual heat for five minutes.

Avocado and Chocolate Cookies

Time: 25mins   **Serves:** 1

INGREDIENTS

- 1tsp. baking powder
- 2/3 cup cocoa powder
- 1/2tsp. salt
- 1/4 cup coconut oil
- 1¼ cups all-purpose flour
- 1/2 cup brown sugar
- 1/3 cup granulated sugar
- 1tsp. vanilla extract
- 1/4 cup avocado
- 1/2 cup chocolate chips
- 1/3 cup almond milk

METHOD

1. Preheat your oven to 350°F, and line a baking sheet with parchment paper.
2. Combine the flour, salt, baking powder, and cocoa.
3. Beat the coconut oil with the avocado and sugars together until creamy, then add the vanilla extract.
4. Combine with the flour, then add the milk and mix to form a dough.
5. Fold in the chocolate chips.
6. Shape into balls and place on your sheet, two inches apart. Flatten.
7. Bake for around ten minutes.

Super Simple Cookies

Time: 45mins   **Serves:** 320

INGREDIENTS

- 9 cups unrefined sugar
- 7lbs. vegan margarine
- 1/4 cup vanilla extract, plus
- 8lbs. all-purpose flour
- 2½tsp. vanilla extract

METHOD

1. Preheat your oven to 400°F.
2. Cream the margarine with the sugar until pale and creamy, then add the vanilla and flour.
3. Dollop onto a baking sheet, and flatten with a fork.
4. Bake for ten to twelve minutes.

Almond Cookies

Time: 40mins   **Serves:** 54

INGREDIENTS

- 180g. all-purpose flour
- 1/4tsp. salt
- 120g. sugar
- 1tsp. baking powder
- 120g. almond meal
- 150ml. vegetable oil
- 1tsp. baking soda

METHOD

1. Preheat your oven to 350°F.
2. Combine the dry ingredients, then add the oil to form a dough.
3. Roll into balls, then put onto lined cookie sheets, 1 inch apart, and bake for fifteen to twenty minutes.

Cupboard-Emptying Cookies

Time: 27mins

INGREDIENTS

- 2tbsp. pumpkin puree
- 1 banana, ripe and mashed
- ¼ cup almond butter
- 1½tbsp. agave nectar
- ½tsp. vanilla extract
- ¾ cup rolled oats
- ¼ cup desiccated coconut
- ¼ cup whole wheat flour
- ¼tsp. baking powder
- 1 pinch salt
- ¼tsp. baking soda
- 3tbsp. pecans, chopped
- ¼ cup semi-sweet chocolate chips
- 1tbsp. raisins

METHOD

1. Preheat your oven to 350°F.
2. Add the peanut butter to the mashed banana, along with the pumpkin puree, baking soda, baking powder, agave nectar, salt, and vanilla.
3. Stir in the oats, desiccated coconut, and flour.
4. Fold in the chocolate chips, raisins, and pecans.
5. Dollop onto a lined baking sheet, and flatten.
6. Bake for fifteen to seventeen minutes.

Cookie Bars

Time: 45mins   **Serves:** 24

INGREDIENTS

- 1tsp. baking soda
- 2¼ cups all-purpose flour
- 1tsp. baking powder
- 1¼ cups brown sugar
- ¼tsp. xanthan gum
- ¼ cup cane sugar
- 1 cup softened vegan butter
- ¾tsp. salt
- 1tsp. vanilla extract
- 10-12oz. vegan chocolate chips
- 2 egg substitute

METHOD

1. Preheat your oven to 375°F, and grease a 9x13 inch pan.
2. Combine the dry ingredients, the mix in the wet ingredients.
3. Fold in the chocolate chips with your hands.
4. Spread the dough out along the base of the pan, then bake for fifteen to seventeen minutes.
5. Once cooled, cut into bars.

Easy No-Bake Cookies

Time: 13mins   **Serves:** 36

INGREDIENTS

- 1½tsp. vanilla
- ½ cup sugar
- ½ cup creamy peanut butter
- ½ cup powdered vanilla coffee creamer
- 3tbsp. brown rice syrup
- ⅓ cup sweetened flaked coconut
- 2 cups small pretzels, crushed

METHOD

1. Whisk the creamer with two tablespoons of water and the vanilla.
2. In a saucepan over a medium heat, melt the peanut butter with the sugar and syrup, then stir in the creamer mix, the pretzels, and the coconut.
3. Dollop onto a greased baking sheet, and leave to cool.

Muesli and Chocolate Chip Cookies

Time: 22mins   **Serves:** 30

INGREDIENTS

- 1 cup muesli
- 2/3 cup applesauce
- 3/4 cup whole wheat flour
- 3/4 cup brown sugar
- 1tbsp. egg substitute, powder (Bob's Red Mill is the best kind)
- 1/2tsp. baking soda
- 3/4 cup semisweet vegan chocolate chips
- 1/2tsp. vanilla extract
- 3tbsp. water

METHOD

1. Preheat your oven to 375°F.
2. Combine everything together, folding the chocolate chips in last.
3. Dollop onto a cookie sheet, and flatten slightly.
4. Bake for ten to twelve minutes.

Sunflower Butter Cookies

Time: 27mins   **Serves:** 20

INGREDIENTS

- 1tsp. baking powder
- 11/4 cups all-purpose flour
- 1/2tsp. baking soda
- 1/4tsp. salt
- 2tbsp. sugar
- 1/3-1/2 sunflower seed butter
- 1tsp. molasses
- 1/2 cup maple syrup
- 1tsp. vanilla extract
- 2-3tbsp. water, as needed
- 2-3tbsp. canola oil

METHOD

1. Preheat your oven to 350°F
2. Sift together all the dry ingredients.
3. Combine all the wet ingredients, then incorporate with the dry ingredients.
4. Dollop onto a lined cookie sheet, then bake for ten to twelve minutes.

Gluten-Free Energy Cookies

Time: 25mins   **Serves:** 24

INGREDIENTS

- 1 cup sunflower seeds, finely ground
- 1/4 cup tapioca flour
- 1 cup brown rice flour
- 1tsp. cinnamon
- 1/2tsp. guar gum
- 1tsp. baking powder
- 1/4tsp. salt
- 1/3 cup maple syrup
- 1/3 cup grapeseed oil
- 2tbsp. applesauce
- 1/4-1/2 cup raisins, chopped
- 1tsp. vanilla

METHOD

1. Preheat your oven to 350°F.
2. Combine the seeds, flours, baking powder, cinnamon, guar gum, and salt.
3. Beat all the wet ingredients together, then combine with the dry ingredients.
4. Fold in the raisins, then mix until it thickens.
5. Roll into balls, then flatten on a greased cookie sheet.
6. Bake for around fifteen minutes.

Gluten-Free, Grain-Free Chocolate Chip Cookies

Time: 22mins   **Serves:** 18

INGREDIENTS

- ½ cup packed pitted Medjool dates
- ¼ cup virgin coconut oil
- ¼ cup hot water
- ¼ cup maple syrup
- 2tsp. vanilla
- ¼ cup ground flaxseeds
- 1 cup almond butter
- ½ cup almond meal flour
- 1 cup quinoa
- ¾tsp. baking soda
- ¼-½ cup mini chocolate chip
- ¼tsp. salt

METHOD

1. Preheat your oven to 350°F, and grease a cookie sheet.
2. Leave the dates to soak in the hot water for five minutes, then tip into a blender with the water, add the coconut oil and maple syrup, and blend until smooth.
3. Transfer to a bowl, then add the ground flaxseeds and vanilla. Beat well, then add the almond butter and beat again.
4. Add the remaining ingredients, then combine.
5. Dollop onto a greased cookie sheet, and gently flatten.
6. Cook for around ten to twelve minutes.

No-Bake Peanut Butter and Oatmeal Cookies

Time: 6mins   **Serves:** 24

INGREDIENTS

- 2 cups sugar
- 4tbsp. cocoa
- ½ cup almond milk
- ½ cup coconut oil
- ½ cup creamy peanut butter
- 2tsp. vanilla
- 3-3½ cups quick-cooking oats

METHOD

1. Put the sugar, cocoa, milk, and peanut butter in a saucepan and bring to a rolling boil for a minute.
2. Remove from the heat and stir in everything else.
3. Dollop onto wax paper, and leave to cool.

Raw Apple Cookies

Time: 24hrs 20mins   **Serves:** 20

INGREDIENTS

- 1 cup agave nectar
- 6 apples, cored and peeled
- 1 ¾ cups almonds, ground
- ¼ cup ground cinnamon
- 1¼ cups raisins

METHOD

1. Slice half of the apples.
2. Blitz the rest of the apples in a food processor, then add the shredded apples to the sliced apples.
3. Add the agave nectar, raisins, ground almonds, and cinnamon to the bowl, and combine.
4. Shape into cookies around three-inches thick, then dehydrate in your dehydrator for 24 hours at 105°.

Quick and Easy Gingerbread Cookies

Time: 25mins

INGREDIENTS

- 1/4 cup dark brown sugar
- 1/2 cup oil
- 1/4 cup dark molasses
- 1/2 cup soymilk
- 1/2 cup white sugar
- 1tsp. vanilla
- 1tsp. baking powder
- 1/2tsp. ginger
- 31/4 cups all-purpose flour
- 1/2tsp. cinnamon

METHOD

1. Preheat your oven to 350°F, and grease baking sheets.
2. Combine your oil, sugars, baking powder, molasses, vanilla, soymilk, and spices.
3. Sift in the flour, kneading as you go.
4. Roll onto a floured surface, then cut into shapes and place on your baking sheets.
5. Bake for eight minutes, then place baking sheets on a towel to cool, not a cooling rack.

Dreamy Sugar Cookies

Time: 35mins   **Serves:** 40

INGREDIENTS

- 11/4 cups sugar
- 1/3 cup vegetable oil
- 2tsp. vanilla extract
- 7tbsp. vegan margarine, softened
- 2tsp. baking powder
- 25 almonds, halved
- 11/2 cups all-purpose flour

METHOD

1. Preheat your oven to 300°F.
2. Cream your margarine, sugar, and vanilla until light and fluffy, then slowly add the oil.
3. Knead in the remaining ingredients.
4. Shape into balls, then press an almond half in each. Place on a lined cookie sheet.
5. Bake for around twenty minutes.

Sally's Semolina Cookies

Time: 20mins   **Serves:** 12

INGREDIENTS

- 1/2 cup all-purpose flour
- 2tsp. baking powder
- 1 cup light brown sugar
- 1/2tsp. salt
- 1/2 cup oil
- semisweet vegan chocolate chips or nuts, for topping
- 11/2 cups semolina flour
- 1/4tsp. allspice
- 1/4 cup water
- 1/2tsp. orange blossom water
- 1tsp. vanilla extract

METHOD

1. Preheat your oven to 350°F.
2. Combine the flours, salt, baking powder, and allspice.
3. Beat the oil, water, sugar, and extracts together, then mix in the dry ingredients.
4. Roll into balls, and line up on a greased baking pan.
5. Push nuts or chocolate into each cookie, then bake for ten minutes.

Fudge-Topped Cookies

Time: 1hr

INGREDIENTS

COOKIES

- 1¼ cups all-purpose flour
- ½tsp. salt
- ½tsp. baking soda
- 14tsp. soymilk, mixed with 1tsp. white vinegar
- ⅓ cup Earth Balance whipped spread

FUDGE SAUCE

- 1 cup chocolate chips
- 4⅓ cups confectioners' sugar, sifted
- 1tbsp. Earth Balance whipped spread

- ½tsp. vanilla
- ½ cup granulated sugar
- 1tbsp. canola oil
- 1 Ener-G Egg Substitute

- 2tbsp. corn syrup
- 1 pinch salt
- 1tsp. vanilla extract

METHOD

1. Preheat your oven to 350°F. Combine the flour, baking soda, and salt.
2. Add the vanilla to the soymilk mix.
3. Cream together the Earth Balance and sugar, then add the prepared egg replacer and oil. Beat well.
4. Mix in the flour and soymilk mixtures and beat until smooth.
5. Dollop onto a baking sheet, and bake for fifteen to seventeen minutes.
   TO MAKE THE FUDGE SAUCE:
1. Melt the chocolate chips and Earth Balance together, then add the confectioners' sugar, vanilla, corn syrup, salt, and six tablespoons boiling water. Thin the icing by adding more water a little at a time, then drizzle all over the cooled cookies.

Snowballs

Time: 50mins   Serves: 43

INGREDIENTS

- 1 cup vegan margarine
- 2tsp. almond extract

- ¼ cup granulated sugar
- 2 cups all-purpose flour

- 2 cups confectioners' sugar
- 2 cups pecans, finely chopped

METHOD

1. Preheat your oven to 300°F.   Cream the sugar with the almond extract and butter until light and fluffy.
2. Mix in the flour, followed by the chopped nuts. Blend well.
3. Roll into balls and place on a cookie sheet, well-spaced.
4. Bake for thirty minutes, then roll in confectioner's sugar while still warm.

Carob Chip Cookies

Time: 20mins

INGREDIENTS

- 1 cup flour
- ¼tsp. salt
- ½tsp. baking soda

- ¼ cup vegan butter
- 1½tsp. Ener-G Egg Substitute
- ½ cup sugar

- 2tbsp. water
- ¾ cup carob chips
- ½tsp. vanilla

METHOD

1. Preheat your oven to 375°F. Combine the flour, baking soda, and salt.
2. Cream the vegan butter with the sugar, vanilla, and egg replacer.
3. Combine the two mixtures, then fold in the carob chips.
4. Dollop onto a lined cookie sheet, and bake for eight to ten minutes.

Oatmeal Spice Cookies

Time: 47mins

INGREDIENTS

- 1 cup grapeseed oil
- 12/3 cups rolled oats
- 1 cup raw sugar
- 1/3 cup mixture of the following
- 1/2 cup orange juice
- 1/3 cup sunflower seeds
- 1tsp. orange rind
- 3 cups whole wheat flour
- 2-3tsp. carrots, finely grated
- 2tsp. baking powder
- 1tsp. salt
- 1tsp. baking soda
- 1tsp. ground cinnamon
- 1/8tsp. ground cloves
- 1/2tsp. ground ginger

METHOD

1. Preheat your oven to 325°F.
2. Cream your grapeseed oil with the cane sugar, then stir in the oats, rice milk, seed-nut mixture, orange juice, orange rind, and carrot.
3. Add everything else, and combine.
4. Dollop onto a cookie sheet, and bake for around twenty minutes.

Maltitol and Chocolate Chip Cookies

Time: 17mins   **Serves:** 15

INGREDIENTS

- 2tbsp. canola oil
- 1/3 cup almond butter
- 3/4 cup maltitol
- 1/3 cup water
- 1/4 cup brown sugar
- 1tsp. vanilla extract
- 3/4 cup whole wheat flour
- 1/4 cup coconut flour
- 1/2tsp. baking soda
- 1/2 cup chocolate chips
- 1 cup oatmeal

METHOD

1. Preheat your oven to 425°F, and grease a large baking sheet.
2. Combine all your ingredients until well incorporated.
3. Dollop onto a cookie sheet, and bake for twelve minutes.

Tahini Oat Cookies

Time: 25mins   **Serves:** 12

INGREDIENTS

- 1 cup whole wheat pastry flour
- 1tsp. baking powder
- 1/4tsp. salt
- 1/4 cup tahini
- 1tsp. vanilla extract
- 1 cup rolled oats
- 1/4 cup sesame oil
- 2tsp. cornstarch
- 2tbsp. sesame seeds
- 1/2 cup maple syrup

METHOD

1. Preheat your oven to 350°F.
2. Grind you oats in a food processor until coarsely ground.
3. Transfer to a bowl, and combine with the flour, salt, and baking powder.
4. Chuck your tahini, vanilla, sesame oil, cornstarch, and maple syrup into your food processor and blend smooth.
5. Combine with the oat mixture.
6. Dollop onto a baking sheet, and sprinkle with sesame seeds.
7. Bake for ten to twelve minutes.

Easy Peasy Chocolate Chip Cookies

Time: 23mins   **Serves:** 12

INGREDIENTS

- 2tsp. cinnamon
- 1¼ cups whole wheat flour
- ½tsp. salt
- ½ cup margarine
- ½tsp. baking soda
- ½ cup turbinado sugar
- 2tsp. vanilla
- ⅓ cup brown sugar
- 1tbsp. molasses
- 8oz. semi-sweet chocolate chips
- ½tsp. water

METHOD

1. Preheat your oven to 350°F.
2. Mix together the flour, salt, cinnamon, and baking soda.
3. Cream the margarine with the sugar until pale, then add the vanilla, molasses, and water.
4. Mix with the dry ingredients, and combine.   Fold in the chocolate chips.
5. Dollop onto a lined cookie sheet, and bake for around ten minutes.

Chunky Chocolate and Walnut Oatmeal Cookies

Time: 40mins   **Serves:** 12

INGREDIENTS

- 2½ cups all-purpose flour
- 1tsp. baking soda
- 2 cups light brown sugar
- 2tsp. canola oil
- 1tsp. salt
- ½ cup soymilk
- 1tsp. cinnamon
- 2tsp. vanilla extract
- 1 cup dairy-free margarine
- 1½ cups rolled oats
- 1 cup dark semisweet chocolate chunk
- 1 cup walnuts, chopped

METHOD

1. Preheat your oven to 350°F.
2. Combine the flour, baking soda, brown sugar, salt, margarine, cinnamon, soymilk, vanilla extract, and canola oil.
3. Stir in the oatmeal, chocolate chunks, and walnuts.
4. Roll into balls, then flatten into cookie shapes on your cookie sheet, spaced apart. Top with more chocolate chunks.   Bake for twelve to fifteen minutes.

Crinkly Chocolate Cookies

Time: 25mins   **Serves:** 16

INGREDIENTS

- 4oz. unsweetened chocolate, melted
- ¼ cup granulated sugar
- 1 cup light brown sugar, packed
- 8oz. firm silken tofu, drained and mashed
- 1tbsp. baking powder
- 2tsp. vanilla extract
- ½tsp. salt
- ½ cup vegan margarine
- 1 cup powdered sugar
- 2 cups all-purpose flour

METHOD

1. Beat together the margarine, chocolate, and sugars until light and fluffy.
2. Add the tofu and beat until well blended.   Stir in the vanilla, baking powder and salt.
3. Add the flour, and combine well.   Cover and chill overnight.
4. Preheat your oven to 350°F, and grease a cookie sheets.
5. Roll into balls, and roll in powdered sugar.
6. Place two inches apart on prepared cookie sheets, and bake for around fifteen minutes.

Ginger Sugar Cookies

Time: 25mins   **Serves:** 12

INGREDIENTS

- ¼lb. vegan margarine, softened
- 1tsp. vanilla
- ¾ cup sugar
- ½tsp. lemon zest
- 1¼ cups flour
- 1tbsp. soymilk
- ⅛tsp. salt
- 2tsp. powdered ginger
- ¼tsp. baking powder

METHOD

1. Preheat your oven to 350°F.
2. Cream the margarine with the sugar until light.
3. Add the vanilla, soymilk and lemon zest, and beat together well.
4. Sift in the dry ingredients, and combine. Roll out onto a floured surface, and cut into cookies.
5. Place an inch apart on a cookie sheet, and bake for eight to ten minutes.

Mega Milano Cookies

Time: 30mins   **Serves:** 16

INGREDIENTS

- ¾ cup sugar
- 2tsp. pure vanilla extract
- ½ cup canola oil
- 1tsp. finely grated orange
- zest
- 2tbsp. cornstarch
- ⅓ cup rice milk
- 2 cups flour
- 1tsp. baking powder
- 6oz. chocolate chips, bittersweet
- ¼tsp. salt

METHOD

1. Preheat your oven to 350°F, and grease two large cookie sheets.
2. Combine the milk, oil, sugar, vanilla, and zest.
3. Add half the flour, along with the cornstarch, baking powder, and salt.
4. Combine, then add the rest of the flour.
5. Shape into Milano biscuits, then bake for around fifteen minutes.
6. Once cooled, dip the bottom of a cookie in melted chocolate, and sandwich with another. Repeat until you've used all your cookies. Leave to set in the fridge for at least an hour.

Chocolate Chip and Tofu Cookies

Time: 25mins   **Serves:** 36

INGREDIENTS

- 2tsp. baking powder
- 1¾-2¼ cups white whole wheat flour
- ¼tsp. salt
- ½ cup turbinado sugar
- 1 cup vegan margarine
- ⅓ cup light brown sugar
- ½ cup pureed extra firm tofu
- ½ cup dark brown sugar
- 1tbsp. vanilla extract
- 2 cups semisweet vegan chocolate chips
- 2tsp. artificial vanilla flavoring

METHOD

1. Preheat your oven to 350°F. Combine the flour, baking soda, and salt.
2. Cream the sugars with the margarine until fluffy. Add the pureed tofu and mix well.
3. Stir in the vanilla, the combine with the flour mix. Fold in the chocolate chips.
4. Bake for ten to fifteen minutes. Freeze remaining dough for munching or cooking on a whim.

Vegan Pies

Super Simple Pumpkin Pie

Time: 1hr 5mins   **Serves:** 10-15

INGREDIENTS

- 3⁄4 cup sugar
- 16oz. can pumpkin puree
- 1⁄2tsp. salt
- 1⁄2tsp. ginger
- 1tsp. cinnamon
- 1⁄4tsp. clove
- 1 9-inch pie shell
- 12oz. soft tofu, processed in blender until smooth

METHOD

1. Preheat your oven to 425°F.   Cream the pumpkin with the sugar, then add the salt, spices, and tofu.
2. Fill the shell, then bake for fifteen minutes.
3. Reduce the temperature to 350°F, and bake for another forty minutes.

Pumpkin Pie

Time: 35mins   **Serves:** 8

INGREDIENTS

CRUST
- 1⁄2 cup unbleached flour
- 1⁄2tsp. salt
- 7tbsp. whole wheat flour, plus more for rolling
- 1⁄2tsp. sugar
- 3tbsp. canola oil
- 1⁄2tsp. baking powder
- 3tbsp. soymilk
- 3-4tbsp. water
- 1⁄2tsp. lemon juice

FILLING
- 1 cup low-fat soymilk
- 2 cups canned pumpkin
- 3⁄4 cup granulated cane syrup
- 1⁄2tbsp. dark molasses
- 1⁄4 cup cornstarch
- 1tsp. vanilla extract
- 1⁄2tsp. salt
- 1tsp. ground cinnamon
- 1⁄2tsp. ground ginger
- 1⁄4tsp. ground allspice
- 1⁄4tsp. nutmeg, freshly grated

METHOD

1. To make the crust, combine the flours, sugar, salt, and baking powder, then add the oil and soymilk to form a dough.   Refrigerate for an hour, then roll onto a floured surface and line a 9-inch pie pan.
2. Cover and refrigerate until ready to use. Pre-heat your oven to 425°F.
3. Blend your filling ingredients until smooth, then pour into the crust.   Bake for ten minutes, then reduce the temperature to 350°F and bake until the filling is set, about fifty minutes.

Traditional Apple Pie

Time: 1hr 25mins   **Serves:** 6

INGREDIENTS

- 1⁄2 cup raisins
- 6 large apples, peeled, cored, and sliced
- 3⁄4 cup maple syrup
- 2tsp. cinnamon
- 1-2tsp. lemon juice
- 2 1⁄2tbsp. cornstarch
- 1-2tbsp. whole wheat flour
- 1 pie crust

METHOD

1. Preheat your oven to 350°F. Boil water in a large pot, and add the apples and raisins.
2. Simmer for ten minutes, then drain, reserving a quarter-cup of the water.
3. Coat the apples and raisins in the maple syrup, cinnamon, and lemon juice.
4. Pop the water into a saucepan, and add the corn starch. Stir until thickened, then add the apples.
5. Stir in the whole wheat flour, then pour into the pie crust, and bake for thirty minutes.

Low-Fat Pineapple Pie

Time: 1hr   **Serves:** 16

INGREDIENTS

BASE

- 2tsp. baking powder
- 250g. all-purpose flour
- 100g. sugar
- 80ml. canola oil
- 80ml. pineapple juice

CREAM

- 250g. soy yogurt, vanilla flavored
- 1tbsp. soy yogurt, vanilla flavored
- 1 fresh pineapple, peeled and chopped
- 100g. cornstarch

METHOD

1. To make the cream, blend the chopped pineapple, yogurt, and cornstarch in a food processor.
2. Tip into a deep saucepan, and heat over medium heat. Stir constantly until thickened, then set aside.
3. Preheat your oven to 180°C.
4. To make the base, combine the flour with the baking powder and sugar, then add the juice and oil to form a dough.
5. Reserve a third of it, then using the bigger part, roll into a half-inch crust.
6. Line your pie pan, prick all over with a fork, and fill with the cream.
7. Roll out the remaining dough, and use to top the pie. Crimp the edges closed, and cut lines in the top to allow the steam to release.
8. Brush with the tablespoon of soy yogurt.
9. Bake for around 45 minutes.

Pecan Pie

Time: 8hrs   **Serves:** 6

INGREDIENTS

- 1-2 cup toasted unsalted pecan halves

FILLING

- 3⁄4 cup water
- 1⁄2 cup brown sugar (packed)
- 3⁄4 cup white sugar
- 3⁄4 cup water
- 1⁄4 cup cornstarch
- 1 pinch salt
- 4 1⁄2tbsp. rum or bourbon
- 1tsp. pure vanilla extract
- 2tbsp. vegan margarine

METHOD

1. Mix the cornstarch with the water.
2. Preheat your oven to 400°F, and bake your crust for three minutes. Reduce the temperature to 350°F.
3. Combine the water and sugars, then boil for five minutes. Add the salt and the cornstarch slurry, and whisk rapidly.
4. Cook over a high heat until thick and clear, then remove from the heat.
5. Stir in the margarine and vanilla until melted.
6. Pour it into your shell, and decorate with pecan halves
7. Bake for around thirty minutes, then leave it to set.

Simple Shepherd's Pie

Time: 11mins   **Serves:** 4

INGREDIENTS

- 1tbsp. coconut oil
- 600g. cooked lentils
- 1 white onion, chopped
- 2 garlic cloves, chopped
- 1 red onion, chopped
- 1tbsp. fresh gingerroot, grated
- 1tbsp. cinnamon
- 1tbsp. cumin
- 1tbsp. maple syrup
- 350g. vegetable stock
- 1 can chopped tomatoes
- 735g. sweet potatoes, peeled, chopped, and boiled
- 100ml. coconut milk
- 1tsp. cumin

METHOD

1. Preheat your oven to 350°F.
2. Melt the coconut oil in a pan, then fry the onions, garlic, ginger, and spices until tender and aromatic.
3. Add the remaining filling ingredients and bring to the boil. Simmer for around thirty minutes.
4. Mash the potatoes with the coconut milk and cumin.
5. Pour the filling into a baking dish, top with the mashed potatoes, and bake for twenty minutes.

Enchilada Pie

Time: 50mins   **Serves:** 6

INGREDIENTS

- 1 medium onion, chopped
- ½ cup frozen corn, thawed, drained
- 10oz. red enchilada sauce
- 12oz. vegetarian ground beef
- 1 can chopped green chilies, drained
- 1tsp. ground cumin
- 1 cup pinto beans, drained
- 1tsp. chili powder
- ¼ cup shredded soy cheese
- 4 flour tortillas for burritos

METHOD

1. Preheat your oven to 350°F.
2. Cook the onion over a medium-high heat until softened.
3. Add the 'beef,' and all but a quarter-cup of enchilada sauce.
4. Stir in the corn and chilies, followed by the cumin and chili powder. Simmer for five minutes.
5. In a baking dish, layer one tortilla with ¾ cup of the beef mix, followed by a third cup of beans. Repeat, until you end on a tortilla layer, then top with the reserved sauce and sprinkle with soy cheese.
6. Bake for thirty minutes.

Fruity Mince Pies

Time: 1hr

INGREDIENTS

PASTRY

- ¼ cup tapioca flour
- 1tsp. xanthan gum
- ¼ cup garbanzo bean flour
- 1 pinch salt
- 4tbsp. coconut palm sugar
- ½ cup white rice flour
- 2oz. Earth Balance vegan buttery sticks spread
- 1tsp. pure vanilla extract
- 1tsp. finely chopped lemon zest
- 2tbsp. cold filtered water

FILLING

- 2tbsp. orange zest
- ¼ cup freshly squeezed orange juice
- ½ cup apple, peeled and grated
- 1tsp. lemon zest
- 1 cup raisins
- ½ cup dried cherries
- ½ cup dried apricot
- ½ cup dried cranberries
- ¼tsp. nutmeg
- ½ cup dried blueberries
- ¼tsp. allspice
- 2tbsp. maple syrup
- 1tsp. cinnamon

METHOD

1. Preheat your oven to 180°C.
2. Grease mini half muffin tins.
3. Combine the flours, xanthan, and salt.
4. Cream together the butter, sugar, and vanilla.
5. Add the dry ingredients until it resembles breadcrumbs.
6. Add a little water at a time, until you form a dough.
7. Knead gently, then wrap and chill for an hour.
8. To make the filling, chuck all the ingredients into your blender, and blend until smooth.
1. Roll out the dough, then line your muffin tins and blind bake for around ten minutes.
2. Add the filling, and bake for another five minutes.
3. Dust with icing sugar to serve.

Mexican Pie

Time: 8mins   **Serves:** 6-8

INGREDIENTS

- 2 cups corn
- 1 can refried beans
- 1tbsp. vegan butter
- cilantro
- Salt and pepper, to taste
- corn tortilla
- ⅓ cup vegan cheddar cheese
- tortilla chips
- green onion
- tomatoes
- ¼ cup ranch dressing

METHOD

1. Mix the beans with a half packet of taco seasoning, and spread half in a pie pan.
2. In a skillet, cook the corn in the butter for two minutes, and season.
3. Top the beans with a layer of ripped up corn tortillas.
4. Next, add half the corn and a sprinkling of cilantro. Season with salt and lime juice.
5. Repeat, then cover with crushed tortilla chips and the cheese.
6. Broil until the cheese is melted, then top with ranch sauce and garnish with the rest of the ingredients.

Yeast-Free Pizza Pie

Time: 49mins   **Serves:** 4-8

INGREDIENTS

- ½ cup wheat bread flour
- ½tsp. salt
- 1 cup spelt flour
- 2tsp. baking powder
- ½ cup water
- 1 can pizza sauce
- Toppings of your choice.
- 2tbsp. olive oil

METHOD

1. Preheat your oven to 400°F.
2. In your food processor, combine the flours, salt, and baking powder.
3. Mix together the olive oil and water together, then pour into the food processor.
4. Blend for another minute, then let sit covered in a damp cloth.
5. Press the crust onto a greased pizza pan, then bake for twelve to fifteen minutes.
6. Top with sauce, then your toppings of choice, and bake for another ten to fifteen minutes.

Pumpkin Whoopie Pies

Time: 36mins

INGREDIENTS

CAKES

- 3 cups all-purpose flour
- 1tsp. baking soda
- 1tsp. baking powder
- 1tsp. salt

- 1tsp. ginger
- 1tsp. cinnamon
- ½tsp. ground cloves
- 1 cup canola oil

- 2½ cups brown sugar
- 2 egg substitute
- 1tsp. vanilla
- 2 cups pumpkin

FILLING

- 4oz. vegan cream cheese
- 2tbsp. vegan butter
- 2 cups powdered sugar

METHOD

1. Preheat your oven to 350°F.
2. To make the cakes, combine the flour, baking soda, baking powder, and spices.
3. Cream the sugar with the oil, pumpkin, egg replacers, and vanilla. Combine this with the dry ingredients.
4. Dollop onto greased cooked sheets, and bake for around fifteen minutes.
5. Meanwhile, make the filling. Beat the cream cheese and butter, then gradually mix in the powdered sugar.   To build, sandwich filling between two cakes.

Very Berry Pie

Time: 45mins   **Serves:** 10-20

INGREDIENTS

- ½ cup brown sugar
- 3 cups berries, of your choice
- 4tbsp. flour
- 1 unbaked pastry for double-crust pie
- 1 pinch salt

METHOD

1. Preheat your oven to 400°F.   Put the berries into your pie crust.
2. Combine the flour and sugar, then sprinkle this all over the berries.
3. Top with the remaining pastry, crimp the edges, and make a few slashes in the op.
4. Bake for around 30 to 35 minutes.

Soy-Free Pumpkin Pie

Time: 1hr 10mins   **Serves:** 8-10

INGREDIENTS

- 1 can pumpkin pie mix
- ½ cup coconut oil, melted
- 2 cups soaked cashews
- ¼tsp. salt
- ½tbsp. lemon juice
- ⅓-½ maple syrup
- pie crust

METHOD

1. Blitz the honey, pumpkin, and oil in your food processor.
2. Add the cashews, salt, and lemon juice, and blend further.
3. Pour into the crust, and allow to set in the freezer.

Chocolate Pie

Time: 25mins

INGREDIENTS

CRUST
- 1½ cups graham cracker crumbs
- 6tbsp. margarine, melted
- ½ cup sugar

FILLING
- 12oz. dark chocolate
- 1tsp. vanilla
- 1lb. silken tofu
- 1-3tbsp. maple syrup

METHOD

1. Preheat your oven to 350°F.
2. To make the crust, mix all the ingredients, then press into a 9-inch pie dish.
3. Bake for twelve to fifteen minutes.
4. To make the filling, blend the tofu until smooth, then add the rest of the ingredients and blend well.
5. Pour into the crust, and freeze for two hours.

Maple and Pecan Pumpkin Pie

Time: 55mins   **Serves:** 8

INGREDIENTS

- 15oz. canned pumpkin
- ½ cup pure maple syrup
- 8oz. silken tofu
- ½tsp. ground ginger
- ¼tsp. nutmeg
- 1tsp. cinnamon
- 1tbsp. flour
- ¼ cup chopped pecans
- 1 pie crust

METHOD

1. Preheat your oven to 350°F.
2. Blend together all but the chopped nuts in your food processor.
3. Pour into the pie shell, then top with the nuts.
4. Bake for forty minutes.

No-Bake Banoffee Pie

Time: 1hr 5mins **Serves:** 8

INGREDIENTS

- 2tbsp. dairy-free margarine
- 300g. graham crackers, crushed
- 350g. silken tofu
- ½ cup soymilk
- ¼ cup maple syrup
- 2 bananas, sliced
- 1tbsp. raw cacao powder
- ½ cup non-dairy whipped topping

METHOD

1. Combine the soymilk, tofu, and syrup in a food processor.
2. Heat for twelve minutes, stirring occasionally, until thicker and caramelized.
3. Layer the crushed grahams in a cake tin, then layer with sliced bananas. Top with the mixture, then leave in the fridge to cool.
4. Once set, spread with whipping cream and sprinkle with cacao powder. Chill for another half hour.

Choca-Mocha Pie

Time: 20mins   **Serves:** 6-8

INGREDIENTS

- 1tsp. agar-agar flakes
- 1 cup water
- 2tsp. instant espresso
- 1 cup maple syrup, fancy grade
- 12oz. firm silken tofu, well-drained
- ¼ cup unsweetened cocoa powder
- ¼tsp. salt
- 1tbsp. vanilla extract
- 1 vegan pie crusts, precooked

METHOD

1. Bring the water and agar-agar flakes to a boil, and simmer for five minutes to dissolve the agar.
2. Add the espresso and stir it until dissolved.
3. In your blender, blitz the tofu, cocoa powder, maple syrup, vanilla, salt, and cooled espresso mixture.
4. Pour into the prepared pie shell, and pop in the fridge to set overnight.

Burrito Pie

Time: 50mins   **Serves:** 8

INGREDIENTS

- 1 can refried beans
- ½ cup salsa
- 1 package tofu
- 1tbsp. taco seasoning
- 1 can re-fried black beans
- 2 cups vegan cheese
- 3 tortillas
- 1tbsp. oil
- ¼ cup vegan mayonnaise
- 1 cup cabbage, chopped
- salt and pepper, to taste

METHOD

1. Preheat your oven to 350°F.
2. Drain the tofu, then crumble into a large pan with a small amount of oil.
3. Stir in the salsa and seasoning, then heat thoroughly.
4. In separate a pan, heat the beans.   Place a tortilla in a pie pan and push the center down.
5. Layer with black beans, then tofu, the refried beans. Sprinkle with cheese, then add the other tortilla and more cheese.
6. Cover in aluminum foil, and bake for thirty minutes.
7. Combine the cabbage with the mayo, then serve with the cooked pie.

Grandma's Banana Cream Pie

Time: 50mins   **Serves:** 8

INGREDIENTS
- 2tbsp. cornstarch
- 14oz. extra firm tofu
- 1 cup raw sugar
- 3 drops yellow food coloring
- 1tbsp. vanilla
- 3 medium bananas
- 1 prepared graham cracker crust
- lemon juice

METHOD
1. Preheat your oven to 375°F.   Drain the tofu and cube it.
2. Slice the banana, and leave to soak in the lemon juice and water for five minutes.
3. In a blender, combine the sugar, tofu, cornstarch, vanilla, food coloring, and drained bananas.
4. Pour into the crust, then bake for 30-35 minutes.
5. Leave to chill in the fridge overnight.

Chocolate and Pumpkin Pie

Time: 1hr 30mins   **Serves:** 8

INGREDIENTS
CRUST
- 1½ cups crumbled vegan chocolate cookies
- 1tbsp. unrefined sugar
- 6tbsp. soy margarine, melted

FILLING
- 1¼ cups semisweet vegan chocolate chips
- 2tbsp. unrefined sugar
- 1 can organic pumpkin pie mix
- 2tsp. arrowroot
- 2tbsp. semisweet vegan chocolate chips
- ⅛tsp. salt

METHOD
1. Preheat your oven to 350°F, and grease a 9-inch pie plate.
2. To make the crust, blend the ingredients then press into the pie plate.
3. Bake for five minutes, then leave to cool. Increase the temperature to 425°F.
1. Melt the chocolate chips.
2. In a food processor, combine the pumpkin pie mix, arrowroot powder, sugar, and salt.
3. Then blend in the chocolate chips.
4. Pour into the crust, and sprinkle with chocolate chips.
5. Bake for fifteen minutes, then reduce heat to 350°F and bake for another 35 minutes.

Tofu-Free Pumpkin Pie

Time: 1hr 5mins

INGREDIENTS
- 1 cup full fat soymilk
- 2 cups solid pack pumpkin
- ¾ cup brown sugar
- 1tbsp. molasses
- ¼ cup cornstarch
- 1tsp. cinnamon
- ½tsp. ginger
- 1tsp. vanilla
- ½tsp. nutmeg
- ¼tsp. allspice
- ½tsp. salt
- Unbaked pie shell

METHOD
1. Preheat your oven to 350°F.   Blend all the ingredients, the pour into your pie shell.
2. Bake for an hour, the leave to set in the fridge overnight.

No-Bake Chocolate Pie

Time: 10mins   **Serves:** 6

INGREDIENTS

- 9oz. semi-sweet chocolate chips, melted
- 12oz. silken tofu
- cinnamon or vanilla flavoring
- 1 graham cracker pie crust

METHOD

Combine all the ingredients in a blender, then pour into your pie crust and pop in the fridge for at least three hours.

Boston Cream Pie

Time: 1hr 10mins   **Serves:** 8

INGREDIENTS

- 1¼tsp. baking powder
- ¼ cup potato (white potato puree)
- ½tsp. salt
- 1tbsp. vegan margarine
- 1tsp. vanilla
- 1 cup confectioners' sugar
- ½ cup sugar
- ¼tsp. lemon extract
- 1 cup unbleached flour
- 1 box vegan vanilla pudding mix
- ½ cup soymilk
- 1½ cups water
- 2tbsp. unsweetened cocoa
- 2tbsp. vegan margarine
- 2tbsp. hot water
- ½tsp. vanilla

METHOD

1. Preheat your oven to 350°F, and grease a cake pan.
2. Prepare the pudding according to package directions. Combine the flour, baking powder, and salt.
3. Cream together the potato and margarine, then add the sugar and beat until fluffy.
4. Add the vanilla and lemon extract, and beat.
5. Gradually add the soymilk and beat until well mixed, then add the flour mixture a little at a time.
6. Pour into the pan, and bake for around thirty minutes. Cool completely.
7. Slice the cake in half horizontally, then fill with vanilla pudding and re-sandwich the cake.
8. Make the glaze by mixing the melted margarine, cocoa, and hot water. Slowly add the confectioner's sugar and vanilla, then pour over the cake.

Lemon Meringue Pie

Time: 8hrs 20mins   **Serves:** 8

INGREDIENTS

- 1 cup sugar
- ¾ cup low-fat silken tofu
- 2 cups water
- 1 vegan pie crusts
- 6tbsp. cornstarch
- 1tbsp. canola oil
- ¼tsp. salt
- ½ cup lemon juice
- 2tsp. finely ground lemon zest

TOPPING

- 2tbsp. pure maple syrup
- ¾ cup low-fat silken tofu,
- crumbled
- 2tsp. hazelnut oil
- 1 pinch ground nutmeg
- 1tsp. vanilla extract

METHOD

1. To make the filling, chuck the water, sugar, tofu, cornstarch, oil, and salt into your food processor.
2. Blend until smooth, the pour into a saucepan.   Bring to a boil, stirring constantly.
3. Once thickened, reduce the heat and stir for another minute.
4. Stir in the lemon juice and zest, then pour into the pie crust.
5. Cover with wax paper, the chill overnight. To make the topping, blend all the ingredients until smooth.
6. Remove the wax paper, then spread the topping over, and serve.

Artichoke Pie

Time: 50mins   **Serves:** 6

INGREDIENTS

- 3tbsp. olive oil
- 1 prepared vegan pie crust
- 1/2 cup onion, chopped
- 3 1/2 eggs replacements (such as Ener-G)
- 2 garlic cloves, minced
- 1 can artichoke hearts, coarsely chopped
- 1tsp. dried basil
- 2tbsp. minced fresh parsley
- 1/4 cup vegan parmesan cheese, grated
- 1 dash Tabasco sauce
- 1/4 cup soymilk
- salt and pepper, to taste

METHOD

1. Preheat your oven to 350°F.
2. Bake your pie crust for ten to fifteen minutes.
3. Meanwhile, heat two tablespoons of the olive oil in a skillet. Cook the onions until softened, then add the garlic and cook for a few minutes more.
4. Combine the egg replacements, onion mixture, and all remaining ingredients bar the olive oil.
5. Fill the pie crust, the top with soy cheese and the rest of the oil.
6. Bake for around thirty minutes.

Coconut Pie

Time: 30mins

INGREDIENTS

- 3 1/2 cups coconut
- 3 cups powdered sugar
- 3lbs. tofu
- 2 vegan graham cracker pie crust
- 6tsp. vanilla
- 1tsp. salt
- 1/2 cup canola oil

METHOD

1. Blend the tofu with the powdered sugar, vanilla, oil, and salt in a food processor until smooth.
2. Fold in three cups of the coconut, the pour into the pie shells and bake for fifteen minutes.
3. Sprinkle the last of the coconut, and bake for another five minutes

Vegan Pizza

Simple Vegan Pizza

Time: 1hr 32mins

INGREDIENTS

CRUST
- 1tsp. sugar
- 1 package active dry yeast
- 2½ cups white flour
- 1 cup warm water

TOPPINGS
- 1oz. fresh basil
- 3 garlic cloves, crushed
- 4tbsp. olive oil
- 3tbsp. ketchup
- 1tbsp. lemon juice
- 2tbsp. pine nuts
- 3 Italian plum tomatoes, sliced
- 1 medium onion, cut in half and sliced
- 2 cups mushrooms, thick sliced

METHOD

1. Mix the water with the yeast and sugar. Leave for ten minutes to activate.
2. Add the flour to the yeast mix and blend well. Allow to rise until doubled, around an hour.
3. Preheat your oven to 450°F. Knock back, and press onto a greased pizza pan.
4. Bake for seven minutes, then turn down the temperature to 350°F.
5. In your food processor, blend the olive oil, garlic, basil, ketchup, pine nuts, and lemon juice.
6. Spread across the crust, then top with the tomatoes, mushrooms, and onions. Bake for ten minutes.

Margherita Pizza

Time: 2hrs 15mins

INGREDIENTS

'MOZZARELLA'
- ¼tsp. salt
- 1tsp. apple cider vinegar
- 1tbsp. nutritional yeast
- 1 cup water
- 1 cup cashews
- 2 garlic cloves, peeled
- 1tbsp. tapioca starch

DOUGH
- 1⅓ cups water
- 4 cups and 2tbsp. all-purpose flour
- 1tsp. salt
- 1tsp. yeast

SAUCE
- 1.5 cans chopped tomatoes
- 1 pinch salt
- 1tbsp. balsamic vinegar
- 1tbsp. olive oil, plus more for drizzling
- 1tsp. dried oregano
- fresh basil, to serve

METHOD

1. Soak the cashews in water overnight, then drain.
2. Blend with the rest of the ingredients in a food processor until smooth. Heat over a medium-low heat until thickened, then pour into a bowl and leave it to thicken further as it cools.
3. To make the dough, mix the water and yeast and leave to activate for ten minutes.
4. Add the flour and salt, the put into an oiled bowl, cover with a damp tea towel, and leave to prove for a couple of hours. To make the sauce, combine all the ingredients.
5. Divide the dough into two, then pat down on a floured surface. Shape it into rough circles, and transfer to a baking sheet.
6. Bake for five minutes, then spread with the sauce and a few dollops of the 'mozzarella.'
7. Drizzle with oil, season, then bake for five to ten minutes. Top with basil to serve.

Tasty Thai Pizza

Time: 27mins   **Serves:** 1-2

INGREDIENTS

- ½ cup vegan Thai peanut sauce
- 1 naan bread
- ½ cup carrot, matchstick sliced
- ¼ cup tomatoes, sliced
- 1 mushroom, sliced
- ¼ cup onion, sliced
- ½ serrano pepper, thinly sliced
- ¼ cup green onion top, sliced
- salt & pepper, to taste

METHOD

1. Preheat your oven to 375°F.
2. Spread the warmed peanut sauce on the flatbread, then layer the vegetables.
3. Top with green onions and season well.
4. Bake for twelve to fourteen minutes.

Very Veggie Pizza

Time: 1hr 30mins   **Serves:** 16

INGREDIENTS

- 2 medium prepared pizza crusts
- ¼ cup pesto sauce
- 15oz. pizza sauce
- 3 cups vegan mozzarella cheese
- ½ cup tomatoes, sliced
- ½ cup yellow tomatoes, sliced
- 1 yellow squash
- ½ small orange bell pepper, diced
- ½ cup red onion, sliced
- 6 fresh mushrooms, sliced
- red pepper flakes
- black olives

METHOD

1. Preheat your oven to 350°F.
2. Spread the pesto sauce and pizza sauce over the pizza dough.
3. Top with half the cheese, then arrange the vegetables over the top.
4. Top with the last of the cheese, and bake for ten minutes.

Mexican Tortilla Pizzas

Time: 25mins   **Serves:** 6

INGREDIENTS

- 2 cans refried beans
- 12 flour tortillas
- 1 cup chopped green bell pepper
- 1 cup taco sauce
- 1 cup chopped red bell pepper
- ½tsp. crushed red pepper flakes
- 6 green onions, sliced

METHOD

1. Preheat your oven to 400°F.
2. Bake your tortillas for three to four minutes, until crisp.
3. Top with the beans, then the taco sauce, then the rest of the toppings. Spread beans evenly over tortillas. Spread taco sauce evenly over beans. Top with ingredients of your choosing.
4. Bake for another seven to eight minutes.

Gluten-Free Taco-Bell Style Pizza

Time: 17mins   **Serves:** 5

INGREDIENTS

- 1 onion, chopped
- 10 corn tortillas
- 1 can refried beans
- 1tbsp. taco seasoning
- 1tsp. olive oil
- 1 Roma tomato, chopped
- 1 cup enchilada sauce
- 1 cup vegan cheese, shredded
- 2 green onions, sliced
- 1 can black olives, sliced

METHOD

1. Cook the onions in the oil, then add the beans and taco seasoning.
2. Spread on the tortillas, then top with enchilada sauce.
3. Divide the remaining ingredients between the tortillas, then broil for a minute or two.

Meat-Free Meat Lovers Pizza

Time: 55mins   **Serves:** 4

INGREDIENTS

CRUST

- 1½tsp. yeast
- 1 cup warm water
- 1tsp. sugar
- 2½-3 cups flour
- ½tsp. salt
- 1tbsp. olive oil
- 1-2tsp. dried Italian herb seasoning
- 1tbsp. garlic, minced

TOPPING

- ¼ medium onion, cut into slivers
- 1tbsp. oil
- 15 vegan pepperoni
- 3-4oz. Gimmie Lean sausage flavor
- ¼tsp. garlic powder
- ⅛tsp. ground fennel
- ¼tsp. basil
- ¼tsp. Italian spices
- ¼tsp. onion powder
- oil
- ¼tsp. red pepper flakes
- 4oz. tomato sauce with basil garlic and oregano
- ¼tsp. garlic powder
- ¼tsp. pizza seasoning
- ¼tsp. Italian spices
- ¼tsp. basil
- 5oz. vegan mozzarella cheese
- ¼tsp. oregano

METHOD

1. Mix the water, sugar and yeast, and leave for five minutes to activate.
2. Add the garlic, oil, and Italian herbs, followed by the flour.
3. Tip onto a floured surface, and knead for around five minutes.
4. Cover, and leave to double in size for around thirty minutes.
5. Knock back, knead a little further, and roll onto a greased pizza pan.
6. Preheat your oven to 425°F.
7. Crisp the pepperoni in oil, then drain on paper towels.
8. Combine the sausage with the spices, and form into small balls. Brown then over a medium-high heat.
9. Spoon the tomato sauce on the crust, the top with the herbs.
10. Add the onions, pepperoni, and sausage.
11. Top with cheese, then bake until golden and the cheese is melted.

Potato Pizza

Time: 1hr 10mins   **Serves:** 8

INGREDIENTS

- 1 can vegetable broth
- 4-5 red potatoes, cubed
- 1 bunch green onion, green and white parts chopped
- 1-2 garlic clove, minced
- 1 large tomatoes, chopped
- 1 pizza crust

METHOD

1. Boil the potatoes and garlic in the broth for around twenty minutes. Mash together with the water.
2. Preheat your oven to 350°F.
3. Spread the potato mixture on the pizza crust, then top with the onion and tomato.
4. Bake for thirty to forty minutes.

Sort-of Cheese Pizza

Time: 35mins   **Serves:** 8

INGREDIENTS

- 1 pizza dough
- 2 garlic cloves
- 1 can tomato paste
- ¼ cup balsamic vinegar
- 1 cup vegan cream cheese (plain)
- 10oz. vegan mozzarella cheese
- Toppings, of your choice

METHOD

1. Preheat your oven to 425°F.
2. Line your pizza pan with the dough.
3. In a blender, blitz the tomato paste, garlic, and vinegar.
4. Spread your cream cheese on the dough, followed by the tomato mixture.
5. Sprinkle with mozzarella, then top with garnishes of your choice.
6. Bake for around twenty minutes.

Sausage, Tomato, and Basil Pizza

Time: 1hr   **Serves:** 4

INGREDIENTS
DOUGH
- 1¼ cups all-purpose flour
- 1tsp. salt
- 1½tsp. active dry yeast
- vegetable oil cooking spray

TOPPING
- ½lb. vegetarian sausage links, cooked and thinly sliced
- 1lb. cherry tomatoes, halved
- 1 cup soy mozzarella cheese, grated
- 1tbsp. balsamic vinegar
- 1tbsp. fresh basil, chopped
- 1tbsp. olive oil
- ½tsp. red pepper flakes
- ½tsp. salt

METHOD
1. Combine the flour, yeast, and salt.
2. Slowly add a half-cup of warm (110 degrees) water until a soft dough forms, then divide into four portions.
3. Roll in balls, grease, and cover with plastic wrap. Leave to rise for around 45 minutes.
4. Once risen, flatten into circles.
5. Preheat your grill to a high heat.
6. Grill each dough circle, for around thirty seconds per side.
7. Divide the toppings between the crusts, cover the grill, and cook for another five to six minutes.

Healthy Pizza

Time: 50mins   **Serves:** 14

INGREDIENTS
- 1 cup brown rice flour
- 1 cup chickpea flour
- 3 cups water
- 2tbsp. sunflower oil
- 8tbsp. sunflower oil
- 2tbsp. ground flaxseeds
- 2tsp. salt
- Toppings of your choice

METHOD
1. Combine the brown rice flour, water, chickpea flour, salt, ground flax, and 2 tablespoons of oil. Blend until thin and smooth.
2. Heat two tablespoons oil on a hot griddle, and ladle four batches of batter onto it, making pancake-sized crusts.
3. Cook for around two minutes per side. Repeat until you're out of batter.
4. Preheat your oven to 400°F.
5. Top your crusts as you like, the bake five to ten minutes.